STEAM

⊢ Tales ⊢
The Secret Garden

Frances Hodgson Burnett

Adaptation by Katie Dicker

WELBECK

Published in 2022 by Welbeck Children's Books
An imprint of Welbeck Children's Limited, part of Welbeck Publishing Group
Based in London and Sydney
www.welbeckpublishing.com

The publishers would like to thank the following sources for their kind permission
to reproduce the pictures and footage in this book. The numbers listed below give
the page on which they appear in the book.

Shutterstock (in order of appearance). Sidhe 6; Studio Barcelona 21; Kalinin Ilya 39;
tersetki 64; Anita Nikitina 106; Makkuro GL 106; Reamolko 120; K3Star 137.

Every effort has been made to acknowledge correctly and contact the source and/or
copyright holder of each picture. Any unintentional errors or omissions will be
corrected in future editions.

ISBN 978 1 78312 847 1

Printed in Dongguan, China

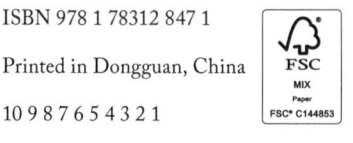

10 9 8 7 6 5 4 3 2 1

Author: Frances Hodgson Burnett
Adaptation: Katie Dicker
Text and design: Tall Tree Ltd.
Editor: Jenni Lazell
Designer: Sam James
Illustrator: Gustavo Mazali
Production: Melanie Robertson

Contents

Chapter 1

A New Home

Everyone said that Mary Lennox was a disagreeable-looking child, with her thin face and sour expression. Mary was born in India. Her father worked for the British government and her mother was a great beauty, but they had no interest in raising a child. Mary spent her days with a nanny and was kept away from her parents as much as possible. Her mother didn't like to hear her crying, so the servants always gave in to Mary's demands. It was no surprise that she grew up to be a selfish child.

When Mary was about nine, she was woken by an unfamiliar servant. "Where's nanny?" she said. "Send her to me!" The woman looked frightened and explained that nanny couldn't come.

Everything was strange that morning. Several servants were missing, and the others scurried by with ashen faces. Mary was left alone, so she wandered into the garden to play. Her mother came onto the veranda with a young officer, and they talked in low voices. Mary noticed the scared look in her mother's eyes.

"Is it so very bad?" Mary heard her say.

"Awfully, Mrs. Lennox, you should have gone to the hills weeks ago."

BRITISH RULE IN INDIA

In the 16th century, Britain joined the race among European countries to claim overseas territories. New lands brought new employment opportunities as well as a plentiful supply of valuable goods.

At its peak in the 1920s, the British Empire covered a quarter of the Earth's land surface. Parts of India fell under British rule in 1858—sometimes called the British Raj ("rule"). India was a source of tea, cotton, indigo, and spices. Indian soldiers also provided a large army (and fought for the British during both World Wars). The British presence in India brought about improvements in infrastructure and education, but it also caused resentment. India gained independence in 1947, when the country was divided into India and Pakistan, and later Bangladesh (1971).

● British Empire at its peak in the 1920s

At that moment, a loud wailing could be heard from the servants' quarters, which made Mary shiver. "It must have broken out among your servants," the officer remarked. And with that, the pair rushed into the house.

Mary discovered that cholera had broken out and people were dying like flies. Mary's nanny had passed away, and three other servants met the same fate that day. The others fled in terror. In all the confusion, Mary hid in the nursery and cried herself to sleep. She slept so soundly, she wasn't disturbed by the wails and scurrying of those around her.

When she woke, the house was perfectly still. She lay waiting for someone to come, but the house just grew more silent. When people had cholera, it seemed they remembered nothing but themselves. Perhaps if they got better, someone would come for her.

Before long, Mary heard men's footsteps and the sound of low voices. "What desolation!" one voice said. "That pretty woman! I suppose the child, too."

Mary was standing in the middle of the nursery when the door opened. The man was startled. "Barney, there's a child here! A child alone! Who is she?"

"I'm Mary Lennox, I fell asleep. Why has nobody come?"

"Poor kid!" the young man called Barney said. "There's nobody left to come."

It was in that strange and sudden way that Mary discovered both her parents had died, and the servants who'd survived had fled.

At first, Mary was taken to an English clergyman's house, but she hated it there and she was so disagreeable that the children wouldn't play with her. It was no surprise then that she was sent somewhere else—to her uncle's house in England. Mr. Archibald Craven lived at Misselthwaite Manor, a desolate old house in the country. "He's a hunchback and he's horrid!" one of the children explained.

Mary was accompanied on the long sea crossing by an officer's wife and was met in London by the housekeeper, Mrs. Medlock, who was a stout woman, with red cheeks and sharp black eyes. Mary didn't like her at all, and it was clear Mrs. Medlock didn't think much of her either.

On their journey to Yorkshire, Mary sat in the corner of the railway carriage. Her black dress made her look yellower than ever, and her limp hair hung beneath her black crêpe hat.

SEA VOYAGE

Mary travels thousands of miles from India to England, leaving the life that she knows behind.

Can you create a papier mâché globe to show just how far Mary travels? Turn to page 14 to find out how.

"I suppose you should be told something," Mrs. Medlock said
reluctantly. "The house is six hundred years old and it's on the edge
of the moor. There are nearly a hundred rooms, although most are
locked. There's a big park around it and gardens and trees. But there's
nothing else," she ended suddenly.

Mary didn't try to look interested.

"Why you're to be kept at Misselthwaite Manor I don't know. *He's* not
going to trouble himself with you, that's for sure. He never troubles
himself with anyone. He's got a crooked back. That set him wrong.
He was a sour young man, until he married."

Mary's eyes turned toward her, despite wanting to show her
indifference. She'd never thought the hunchback would be married
and was a little surprised.

"She was a sweet, pretty thing and he'd have walked the world over to
give her what she wanted. Nobody thought she'd marry him, but she
did, and people said she married him for his money. But she didn't.
When she died it made him stranger than ever. Most of the time he
goes away, or he shuts himself up in the West Wing."

Mary suddenly felt sorry for Mr. Craven. It sounded like something in a book—a man with a crooked back who shut himself away!—it didn't make her feel cheerful at all. She stared out of the window with her lips pinched together as the rain began to pour down the glass.

"You mustn't expect to see him," Mrs. Medlock went on. "And there won't be people to talk to. You'll have to play by yourself. You'll be told what rooms you're allowed to go into. There are gardens enough. But when you're in the house, don't go wandering and poking about. Mr. Craven won't have it."

"I shan't want to go poking about," said Mary, and she stopped feeling sorry for Mr. Craven and began to think he deserved his luck.

Soon Mary was lulled by the splashing of the rain on the window and her eyes grew heavy. It was dark when she woke. Mrs. Medlock was shaking her. "We're at Thwaite Station! We've a long drive ahead."

As they drove off in a smart horse-drawn carriage, Mary was curious about her surroundings. Before long, the horses began to go more slowly, and there seemed to be no more hedges or trees.

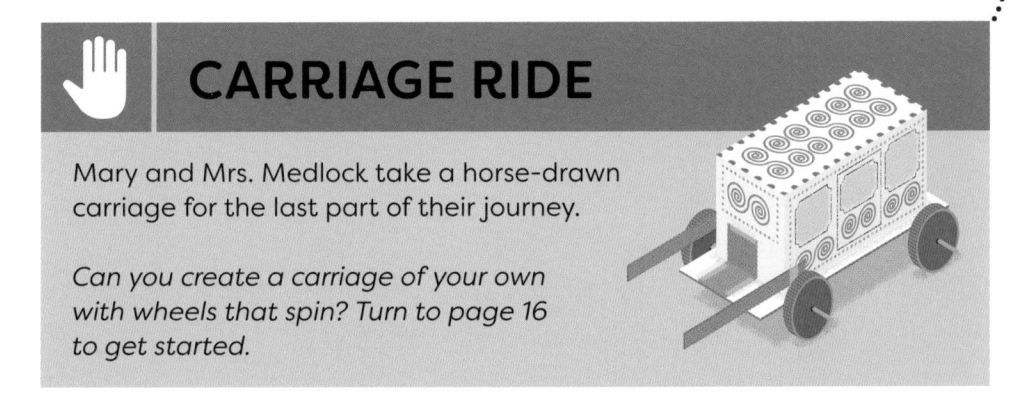

✋ CARRIAGE RIDE

Mary and Mrs. Medlock take a horse-drawn carriage for the last part of their journey.

Can you create a carriage of your own with wheels that spin? Turn to page 16 to get started.

HORSE AND CARRIAGE

Before cars were mass-produced and made affordable, the horse and carriage was the most common type of local transport.

The invention of the "wheel and axle" system made transportation easier. At first, two-wheeled chariots were favored for their strength and speed. These were particularly popular with the Ancient Egyptians, who used them for warfare. Later, four-wheeled carriages were used for heavier loads. The quickest of all were "stagecoaches" pulled by teams of horses. At each "stage" of a long journey, tired horses were replaced with fresh, quicker horses, for maximum speed.

Axle

Wheel

Brougham carriage

Mary could see nothing but a dense darkness on either side.

The horses were climbing up a hilly piece of road when Mary first saw a light. "That's the lodge window," Mrs. Medlock explained. "We'll get a cup of tea soon." Eventually, they stopped before a large, imposing house. It was completely dark, except for a dull glow from an upstairs window.

The huge oak front door opened into an enormous hall. It was so dimly lit Mary didn't want to look at the faces in the portraits and the figures in the suits of armor.

"You're to take her to her room," an old man said in a husky voice. "He doesn't want to see her. He's going to London in the morning."

"Very well, Mr. Pitcher," Mrs. Medlock said, as she led Mary up a broad staircase and down a series of corridors and steps to a fire-lit room with supper on the table. "Here you are! This room and the next are where you'll live—and you must keep to them!"

When Mary woke the next morning, a young housemaid was lighting the fire and raking out the cinders. Mary watched her for a while.

"What's that?" she asked, pointing to the great stretch of barren land through the window.

The young housemaid, Martha, explained it was the moor, and that Mary would get used to its bareness and come to love the spring gorse and broom and heather in flower. "Eh! I wouldn't live away from th' moor for anythin'," she said.

Martha was a round, rosy, good-natured girl with a sturdy way about her, quite unlike the servants Mary was used to in India. She was Mrs. Medlock's servant who'd been sent to help. "Not that you'll need much waitin' on," she said, as she found some clothes Mr. Craven had bought for Mary in London. She pulled out a coat, a hat, and a pair of stout boots so she could play outside.

"If th' goes round that way tha'll come to th' gardens," she said, pointing to a gate in a wall of shrubbery. She seemed to hesitate a second before adding, "One of th' gardens is locked. No one has been in it for ten years."

"Why?" Mary asked. Another locked door to add to the hundred in the house.

"Mr. Craven had it shut when his wife died so sudden. He won't let no one go inside. It was her garden. He locked th' door an' dug a hole and buried th' key. Oh, there's Mrs. Medlock's bell ringing—I must run!"

MAKE A PAPIER MÂCHÉ GLOBE

Mary travels more than 4,750 miles (7,600 kilometers) from India to England, to stay with her uncle. Create your own globe to follow her journey!

1

Inflate your balloon to a spherical shape and tie. Sit your balloon on the small bowl to stop it from rolling away.

YOU WILL NEED:

- punch balloon
- 2 bowls (small and large)
- wooden spoon
- cup of flour
- cup of water
- newspaper
- scissors
- marker
- acrylic paint (blue and green)
- paintbrush

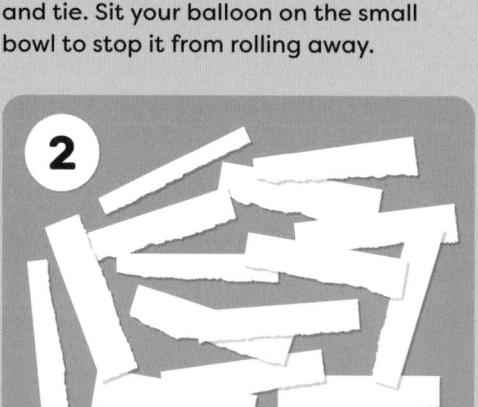

2

Cut your newspaper into strips.

3

FLOUR

In the large bowl, mix the flour and water to make a paste.

4

Dip the newspaper strips into the paste. Apply them to the surface of your balloon.

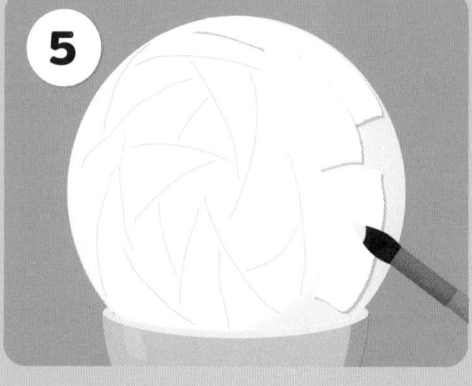

5

Repeat until the balloon is completely covered. Add a second layer. Use the balloon's elastic tie to hang your papier mâché globe up to dry.

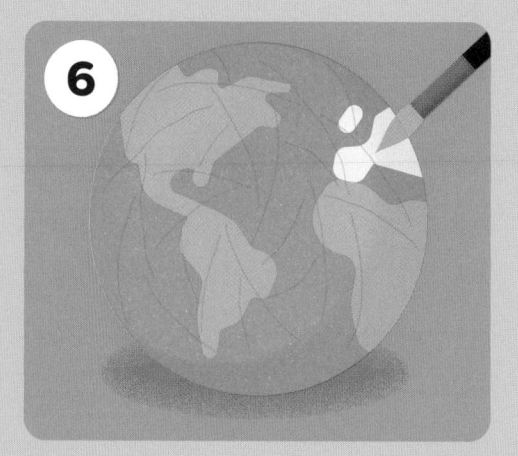

6

When the globe is dry, sit it on the small bowl again. Outline the continents with your marker and paint the blue oceans and green land.

WHY IT WORKS

The flour and water paste acts like a glue. When you add strips of newspaper to your balloon, the paper molds to the shape of the balloon. The paper hardens as it dries. Adding a second layer of newspaper makes this structure stronger. Don't worry if your globe isn't a perfect sphere—neither is planet Earth! When Earth spins in space, forces cause our planet to be slightly squashed at the poles and slightly swollen at the equator.

MAKE A CARRIAGE

Mary and Mrs. Medlock travel across the moor in a horse-drawn carriage. Create a carriage of your own for a windswept journey.

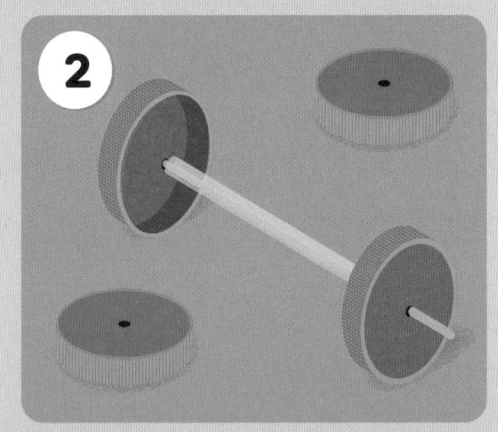

1

Cut the straw in half and thread each half over a skewer. These are your axles.

YOU WILL NEED:

- paper straw
- scissors
- 2 small wooden skewers
- 4 circular plastic lids (all the same size)
- cardstock
- single and double-sided tape
- small cardboard box or margarine tub
- marker pens

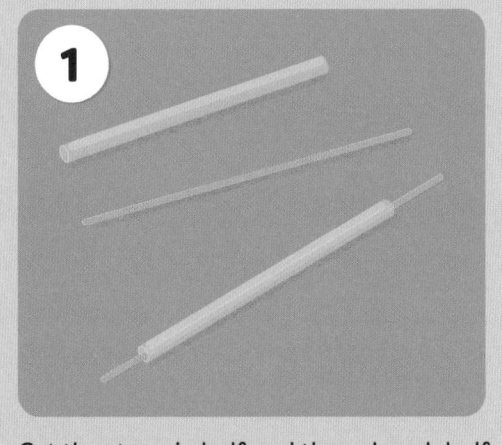

2

Ask an adult to pierce the plastic lids and help you attach the lids to either end of each skewer. These are your wheels.

3

Cut out a rectangle of cardstock that fits comfortably between the wheels as an undercarriage. Tape the straws to it at either end. Check the wheels move freely.

4

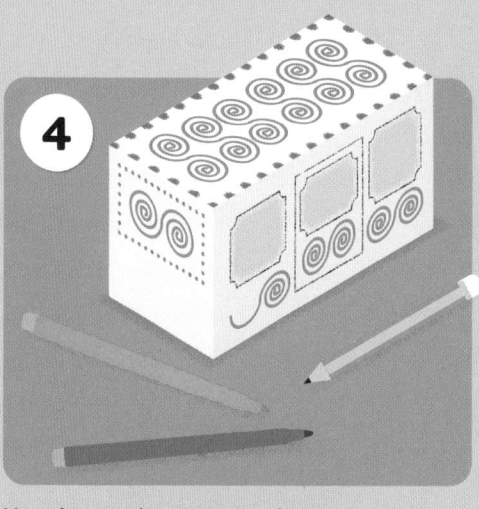

Use the marker pens to decorate your small cardboard box (or tub) with windows and a door for your carriage compartment.

5

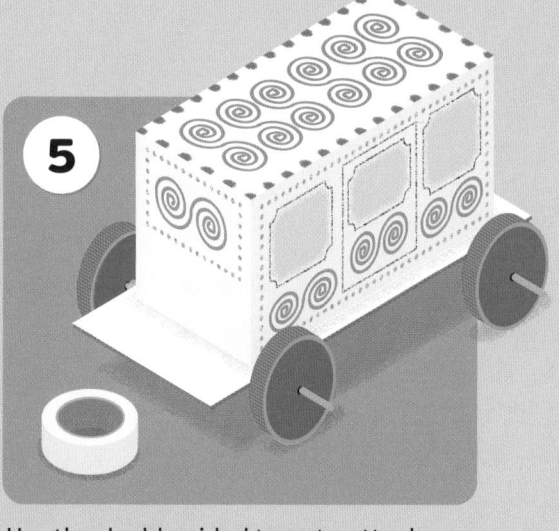

Use the double-sided tape to attach your carriage compartment to the undercarriage.

6

Cut out a rectangle of cardstock and fold in half. Tape this to the front of the carriage as a seat. Add two strips of cardstock on either side, for the shafts.

WHY IT WORKS

When you move a heavy load, the friction between the load and the ground makes it difficult to push or pull. With a "wheel and axle" system, friction between the load and the ground is reduced and it takes less energy to move. The larger the wheel, the easier it is to move the load as the larger diameter creates a greater pulling or pushing force.

Chapter 2

The Cry in the Corridor

Mary ventured into the great gardens, with their wide lawns and winding paths. She found several walled gardens opening into one another. An old man with a spade looked startled when he saw her, and then touched his cap. He didn't seem at all pleased to see her, but Mary felt the same.

She made her way into the orchard and noticed the wall seemed to extend into another garden beyond, but there was no door. She could see the tops of trees, and a robin on one of the branches suddenly burst into song, as if calling her. She loved his cheerful, friendly little whistle.

Mary went back to the old man digging. "There's no door into the other garden," Mary said.

"What garden?" he replied in a rough voice, stopping for a moment.

"On the other side of the wall," answered Mary. "There are trees there, and a robin singing."

To her surprise, a slow smile spread over the gardener's face. He turned and gave a low, soft whistle. Almost at once, Mary heard a soft rushing flight through the air—and the robin flew down near the gardener's foot.

"Here he is," chuckled the old man, and he spoke to the bird as if he were speaking to a child. "Where has tha' been, you cheeky thing."

The bird tilted his tiny head and looked up at him with his soft bright eyes. He seemed quite tame and not at all afraid.

"Art tha' th' little girl from India?" the old man asked. Mary nodded.

"What's your name?" Mary asked. "Ben Weatherstaff," he answered, and then he added with a chuckle as he jerked his thumb towards the robin, "He's th' only friend I've got."

Mary would have liked to ask more questions, but the robin flew away. "He's flown over the wall!" Mary cried out, watching him. "He's flown into the garden where there's no door!"

"He lives there," said Ben Weatherstaff.

"There must be a door somewhere." Mary said.

✋ ATTRACTING ATTENTION

The sound of the robin attracts Mary's attention as if he is calling to her.

Can you make a bird whistle that sings?
Turn to page 28 for some simple instructions.

BIRD SONG

The sound of bird song is a sure sign that spring has sprung. Birds sing during the breeding season to attract a mate and to mark their territory. Scientists think many birds are born with the ability to sing a simple song, although they listen and learn it, too.

Songbirds have a two-sided "voice box" called a syrinx. It is found where the windpipe divides and is used with air from each lung. This enables the songbird to sing two different pitches at the same time.

Birds also use shorter calls, chirps, trills, and warbles to communicate. They may be warning other birds of danger, keeping track of family and friends, or indicating a source of food. Birds use their behavior and body language to communicate as well. Some birds use non-vocal sounds. Woodpeckers, for example, tap or "drum" on trees to communicate.

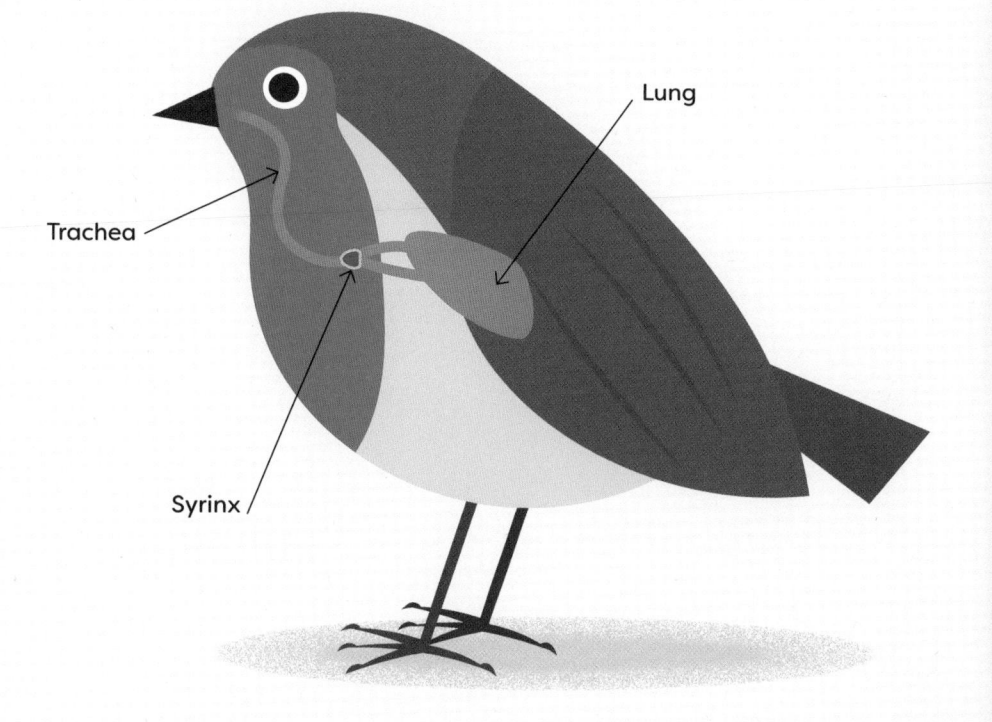

Lung

Trachea

Syrinx

"There was ten year' ago, but there isn't now," the man said abruptly. "None as anyone can find, an' none as is anyone's business. Don't you meddle now and poke your nose where it's not wanted. Here, I must get on with my work. Be gone, and play. I've no more time." And with that, Ben Weatherstaff walked off, without saying goodbye.

Mary tried to get out most days and found herself going to one place more than any other—the long walk outside the walled gardens. She was just looking at one part of the wall where the ivy was bushier when she saw a flash of scarlet and heard a brilliant chirp. There on top of the wall perched the robin, with his head on one side. Then he swooped up to a tree—the same tree Mary had seen him on that first day. "It's in the garden no one can go into," she said to herself. "How I wish I could go inside!"

Mary stayed outside nearly all day and had a big appetite at supper. "Why did Mr. Craven hate the garden?" she asked Martha.

TESSELLATING TRIANGLES

Over ten years, the ivy has grown so thick along the garden wall, it has obscured the door to the secret garden.

Try tessellating some triangles to create an ivy curtain of your own. Turn to page 30 for more details.

CLIMBING PLANTS

Like other vines and creepers, ivy is a climbing plant that grows quickly up the sides of walls, fences, and buildings.

Climbing plants have weak stems, so they need to grow with the help of external support. They grow quickly because all their energy goes into lengthening their stems instead of thickening them. Ivy has a dense evergreen foliage. It produces special roots along its stems, which become lodged in rough surfaces, such as the bark of a tree or a brick wall. Other climbing plants twist their slender stalks around the stems of other plants, as they try to grow toward the light. After ten years of ivy growth, it's no surprise the door to the secret garden has become obscured.

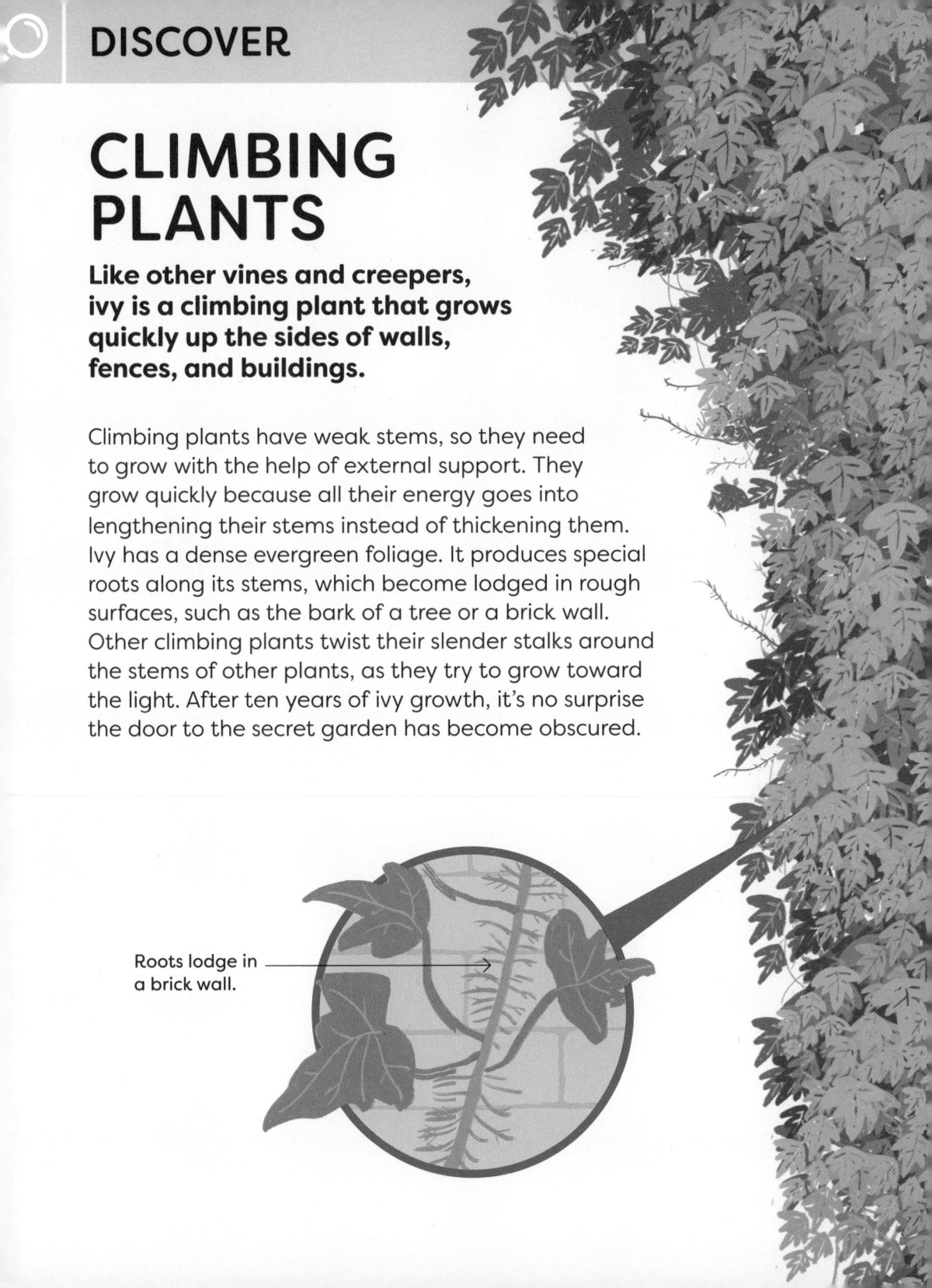

Roots lodge in a brick wall.

"I knew tha'd be thinkin' about tha' garden," she said. "That was just the way with me when I first heard about it."

The wind was howling around the house, but Mary felt safe and warm by the red coal fire.

"It was Mrs. Craven's garden that she made when they were first married an' they'd stay there for hours, readin' and talkin'. She was just a girl an' there was an old tree with a branch bent like a seat. An' she made roses grow over it an' she used to sit there. But one day, th' branch broke an' she fell on th' ground an' was hurt so bad that next day she died. Th' doctors thought he'd go out o' his mind an' die, too. That's why he hates it. No one's ever gone in since, an' he won't let anyone talk about it."

Mary didn't ask any more questions. Her heart was full of sorrow for Mr. Craven. She sat still by the fire, listening to the wind howling. And then she heard a curious sound—almost as if a child was crying somewhere. Perhaps it was the wind itself, but no, she felt sure this sound was inside the house. "Do you hear someone crying?" she said.

Martha suddenly looked confused. "No," she answered, "it's th' wind. Sometimes it sounds like someone's lost on the moor an' wailin'."
"But listen," Mary said. "It's in the house—down one of those long corridors."

At that very moment, a door must have been opened downstairs, for a great draught threw open the door to their room with a crash. They both jumped and the crying sound could be heard more clearly than ever.

"There!" said Mary. "I told you! It's someone crying."

Martha ran to the door and locked it. "It was th' wind," she said stubbornly. "An' if it wasn't, it was probably Betty Butterworth, th' scullery-maid. She's had toothache all day."

But there was something awkward about Martha's manner that made Mary stare very hard at her. She didn't believe a word she was saying.

The next day, the rain poured down and the moor was almost hidden by gray mist and cloud. There could be no going out today.

"What do you do in your cottage when it rains like this?" Mary asked.

"Try to keep from under each other's feet mostly, with fourteen of us," Martha replied. "My brother Dickon doesn't mind th' wet. He says he sees things on rainy days that don't show when it's fair weather. He once found an orphan fox cub and brought it home. He found a half-drowned young crow another time an' tamed it."

Mary loved listening to Martha's tales. "If I had a crow or a fox cub I could play with it," Mary said. "But I have nothing."

"Can tha' read?" Martha asked.

"I haven't any books," said Mary. "Those I had were left in India."

"That's a pity," said Martha. "If Mrs. Medlock'd let thee go into th' library, there's thousands o' books there."

Mary didn't ask where the library was because she suddenly had an idea. She didn't care much for the library itself, but it made her think of the hundred rooms with closed doors. She wondered if they were all really locked and what she'd find if she could get into them. It would be something to do on this wet morning.

Mary wandered about upstairs and down, through long corridors and narrow passages. People must have lived in all these rooms once, but it all seemed so empty, she couldn't believe it was true. She saw so many rooms that she became quite tired. They all had old pictures or tapestries, and curious pieces of furniture and strange ornaments, too.

Mary had wandered about long enough to feel too tired to wander anymore. She lost her way two or three times, by turning down the wrong corridor, but at last reached her own floor again. She was just working out her bearings when the stillness was broken by a sound. It was another cry, but not quite like the one she'd heard last night.

It was the muffled sound of a fretful, childish whine.

"It *is* crying!" Mary's heart began to beat faster, and in her nervous excitement, she grasped the tapestry near her and then sprang back, feeling quite startled. The tapestry was covering a door, which fell open and showed another part of the corridor behind it. Mrs. Medlock was approaching with a bunch of keys in her hand and a very cross look on her face.

"What are you doing here?" she said, taking Mary by the arm and pulling her away. "What did I tell you?"

"I turned the wrong way," Mary explained. "I didn't know which way to go, and I heard someone crying."

She quite hated Mrs. Medlock at that moment, but she hated her more the next.

"You didn't hear anything of the sort," said the housekeeper. "You come along back to your own nursery, or I'll box your ears." She took her by the arm and half pushed, half pulled her up one passage and down another until she reached her room.

"You stay where you're told, or you'll find yourself locked up." As Mrs. Medlock slammed the door behind her, Mary sat on the hearthrug, pale with rage.

"There *was* someone crying—there *was*!" she said to herself.

She'd heard it twice now, and she was desperate to find out who it was!

MAKE A BIRD WHISTLE

The robin sings to Mary and Ben Weatherstaff and seems to be trying to communicate with them. Make a bird whistle of your own to attract attention.

1

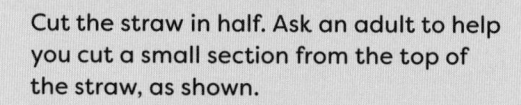

Cut the straw in half. Ask an adult to help you cut a small section from the top of the straw, as shown.

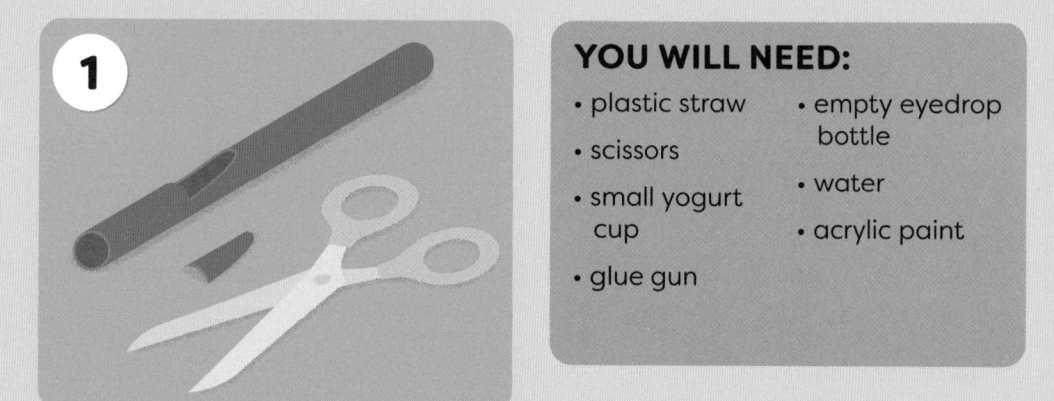

YOU WILL NEED:

- plastic straw
- scissors
- small yogurt cup
- glue gun
- empty eyedrop bottle
- water
- acrylic paint

2

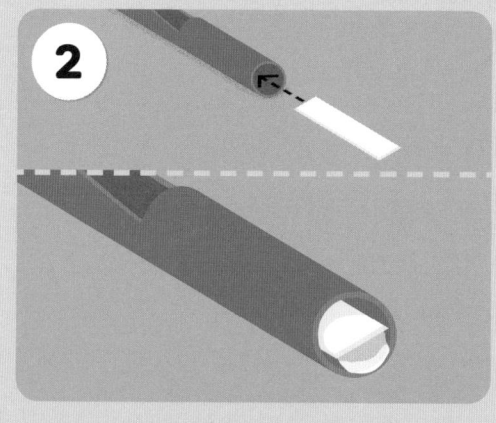

Cut a small piece from the yogurt cup and push it into the straw. Use the glue gun to fill the space beneath the plastic.

3

Once the glue has dried, test your whistle.

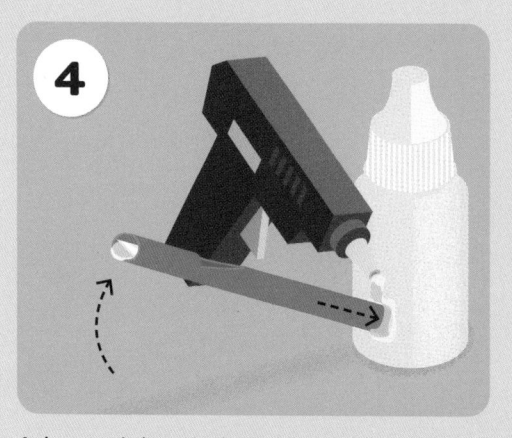

4

Ask an adult to help you make a small hole in the bottom of the eyedrop bottle. Insert the straw whistle and glue in place, tilting slightly upward.

5

Once the glue has dried, half fill the bottle with water. Remove the outer lid so there's an air hole at the top of your bird whistle. Cut a small piece of plastic for the beak and glue in place.

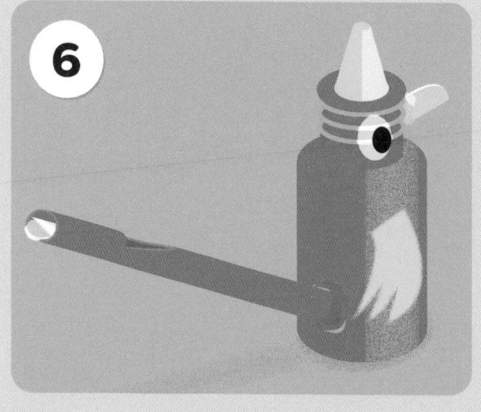

6

Paint your bird whistle with bright colors. Once dry, blow into the whistle to let your bird sing. Cover the lid to see how the sound changes.

WHY IT WORKS

The straw whistle makes a high-pitched sound because you are forcing air through a small hole. Adding the straw to the eyedrop bottle changes the length and sound of the whistle. When the bottle is half-filled with water, blowing the whistle causes the shape and area of the air inside the bottle to change, producing different sounds. Covering the lid from time to time also changes the length of the whistle, just like a wind instrument.

CREATE AN IVY CURTAIN

The door to the secret garden has become obscured by a thick covering of ivy. Can you tessellate some ivy leaves to keep a door hidden, too?

1

Use your pens to draw an old garden wall on your sheet of paper, with a wooden door in the center.

YOU WILL NEED:

- sheet of printer-size paper
- pencil and ruler
- marker pens
- green cardstock
- scissors

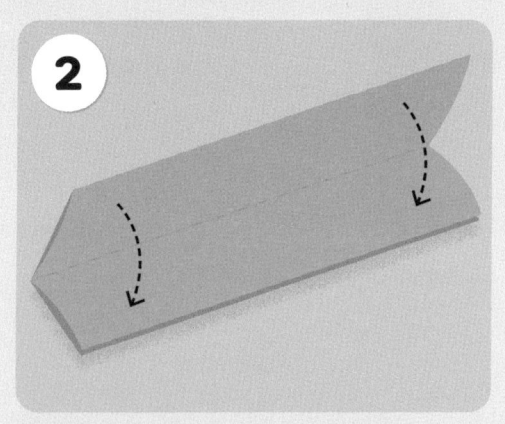

2

Fold your green cardstock in half lengthways, and in half again.

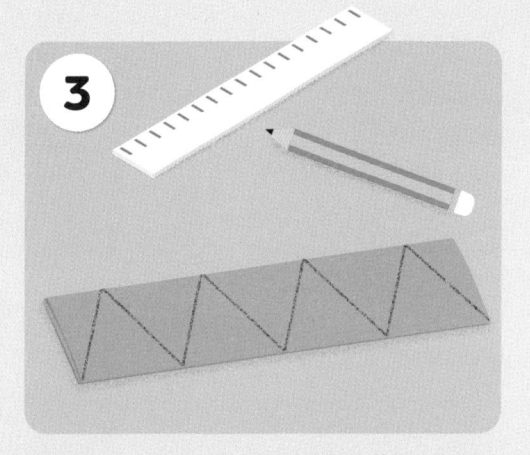

3

Using your ruler, draw a series of isosceles triangles (triangles with two sides of equal length) along your strip of cardstock. These will represent your ivy leaves.

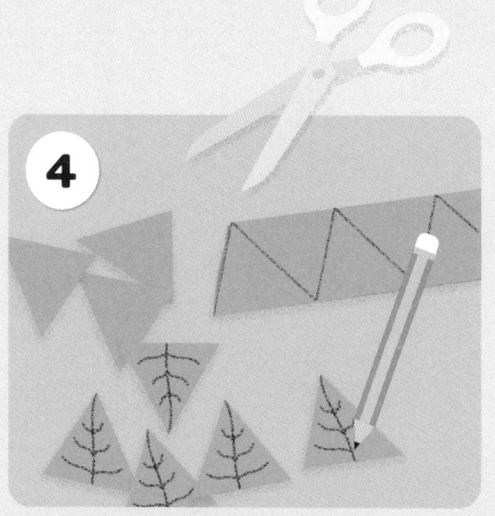

4

Cut out your ivy leaves and draw veins on them with your pencil.

5

Start covering your picture with the ivy leaves. Can you arrange the triangles so they completely cover the surface, without leaving any gaps?

6

Now try a different arrangement, starting in the center, as shown. Which design works best? How many ivy leaves do you need to cover your picture?

WHY IT WORKS

We say that a shape tessellates if we can use it to cover a flat surface without any gaps. All triangles tessellate because the sum of the angles of any triangle add up to 180° (a straight line). You will find that tessellating the ivy leaves in rows will be more effective (and use more leaves) than radiating out from the center.

Chapter 3

The Key to the Garden

Two days later, the rain had stopped, and the gray mist and clouds had been swept away by the wind. It was calm now and a brilliant, blue sky arched over the moorland.

Mary went out as soon as she could. Ben Weatherstaff was working in the first kitchen-garden with two other gardeners.

"Springtime's comin'," he said.

Very soon, she heard the soft rustling of wings and knew at once that the robin had come again. He hopped about so close to her and put his head on one side.

"Do you think he remembers me?" she asked Ben Weatherstaff.

"Remembers thee!" Weatherstaff said indignantly. "He's bent on findin' out all about thee."

Mary made her way to the long ivy-covered wall, when she heard a chirp and saw the robin again pecking about in the soil. "You do remember me!" Mary cried out. She was so happy when he let her come close to him, that she scarcely dared to breathe.

The robin stopped to look for a worm where a dog had been digging and the soil was fresh. When Mary looked down, she saw something almost buried there—a ring of rusty iron or brass. She picked it up. It was an old key which looked like it had been buried a long time.

"Perhaps it's the key to the garden!" she whispered. Mary turned it over in her hands. All she could think about now was finding the door. She decided to carry the key whenever she went out, so she'd be ready.

Martha returned from an overnight visit to her family. "Eh! They did like to hear about you," she said. "They wanted to know all about th' ship you came in. I couldn't tell 'em enough. Oh, and I've brought thee a present! Mother saw it and thought of you, and I'd brought my wages." She pulled a skipping rope from under her apron. Mary gazed at it with a mystified expression. "What's it for?" she asked curiously.

"For!" Martha cried. "Does tha' mean they've not got skippin' ropes in India! This is what it's for, just watch me." Martha began to skip in the middle of the room while Mary looked on with delight. "You just try it," urged Martha, handing her the rope. "If you practice, you'll soon get the hang of it."

Mary liked skipping so much she didn't want to stop. She put on her coat and hat and was making for the door when she turned back slowly. "Martha," she said holding out her hand, "your mother used your wages. Thank you." She said it stiffly because she wasn't used to thanking people. Martha gave her hand a clumsy little shake, as if she wasn't accustomed to it either. Then she laughed.

MIST AND FOG

When the mist comes down, the moor is almost hidden from view. Mist forms when water particles become suspended in the air.

When air cools rapidly, water vapor in the air turns into tiny water droplets. This often happens at night when Earth's heat is lost into space and the ground cools the air closest to it. Fog is denser than mist and less easy to clear in light winds.

In some parts of the world, where water is scarce, "fog catchers" are used to collect water droplets in the air. The water vapor condenses on the surface of a net and runs down to a collecting chamber, a bit like the water droplets you see on a spider's web outside on a chilly day.

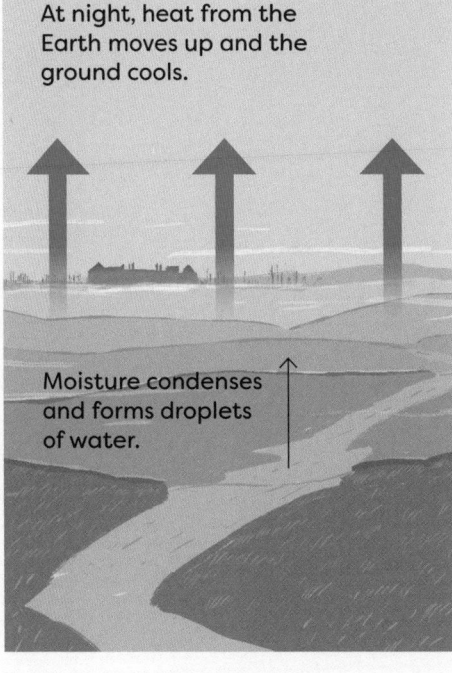

At night, heat from the Earth moves up and the ground cools.

Moisture condenses and forms droplets of water.

You can create your own mist when your warm breath meets cold air.

Mary skipped into the kitchen-garden and saw Ben Weatherstaff digging and talking to his robin. He lifted his head and looked at her with a curious expression. She'd wondered if he'd notice. She really wanted him to see her skip.

"Well!" he exclaimed. "Tha's skipped red into thy cheeks as sure as my name's Ben Weatherstaff. I wouldn't have believed th' could do it."

Mary tried to skip the whole length of the ivy wall but stopped when she got hot and breathless. And there, lo and behold, was the robin swaying on a long branch of ivy. He'd followed her and greeted her with a chirp. "You showed me where the key was yesterday," she said. "You ought to show me the door today!"

 **UNLOCKING SECRETS**

Mary finds that the buried key is a perfect fit for the garden door!

Try making a combination lock of your own for your secret treasures. Turn to page 42 to discover how.

The robin sang a loud, lovely trill to show off. Mary had heard a great deal about Magic in her nanny's stories, and she believed what happened next was pure Magic.

A little gust of wind rushed down the walk, stronger than the rest—strong enough to sway the trailing ivy hanging from the wall. Mary jumped toward it and caught the ivy in her hand, for she'd seen something beneath it— a round knob covered by leaves, a doorknob!

Mary began to pull the leaves aside. Her heart was thumping, and her hands shook with excitement. Her fingers reached the lock of the door which had been closed for ten years. The key fitted the keyhole and turned. It took two hands to do it, but it did turn! Mary took a long breath and looked behind to see if anyone was coming. She held back the ivy as she pushed open the door, which opened ever so slowly. As she shut the door behind her, she stood with her back against it, breathing fast with excitement and wonder and delight. She was standing *inside* the secret garden!

It was the sweetest place anyone could imagine. The high walls were covered with the leafless stems of climbing roses. The ground was covered with brown tufts of grass and bushes.

There were other trees in the garden, too, with climbing roses all over them. There were neither leaves nor roses on them now, and Mary did not know whether they were dead or alive.

"How still it is!" she whispered. She waited a moment and listened to the stillness. "I'm the first person who's spoken in here for ten years."

If Mary had been Ben Weatherstaff, she'd have known whether the wood was alive by looking at it, but she could see only gray and brown branches and no signs of life.

Mary skipped around the whole garden. She thought she saw some little pale green shoots in the soil and knelt down to look at them. "They're tiny growing things," she whispered. "It isn't a dead garden. Even if the roses are dead, there are other things alive."

The grass seemed so thick in some places that she thought the green shoots didn't have enough room to grow. She found a sharp piece of wood to dig and weed out the grass until she'd cleared the space around them. She worked hard until lunchtime and dozens of the pale green shoots were now looking twice as cheerful as they'd been when the grass was smothering them.

"I shall come back this afternoon," Mary said, slipping back through the door. Later, she asked Martha about the green shoots with an onion-like root. "They're bulbs," Martha replied. "Lots o' spring flowers grow from 'em. Eh! Dickon's got a whole lot of them in our garden."

FLOWER BULBS

Some flowers, such as daffodils and snowdrops, produce bulbs—a type of underground stem.

After they flower, the plant absorbs nutrients from the soil and energy from the Sun, which they store in the stem. With lots of food, the plant rests underground during the cold winter until the conditions are right to grow again the following year.

During the winter, the bulb grows underground, sending its roots into the soil. When the temperature conditions are right again, the bulb grows a green shoot, which develops into a stem and eventually flowers, and then the foliage dies down and the cycle begins again.

Some bulbs are grown for food, such as onions and garlic, while others are grown for their decorative flowers, such as daffodils and tulips.

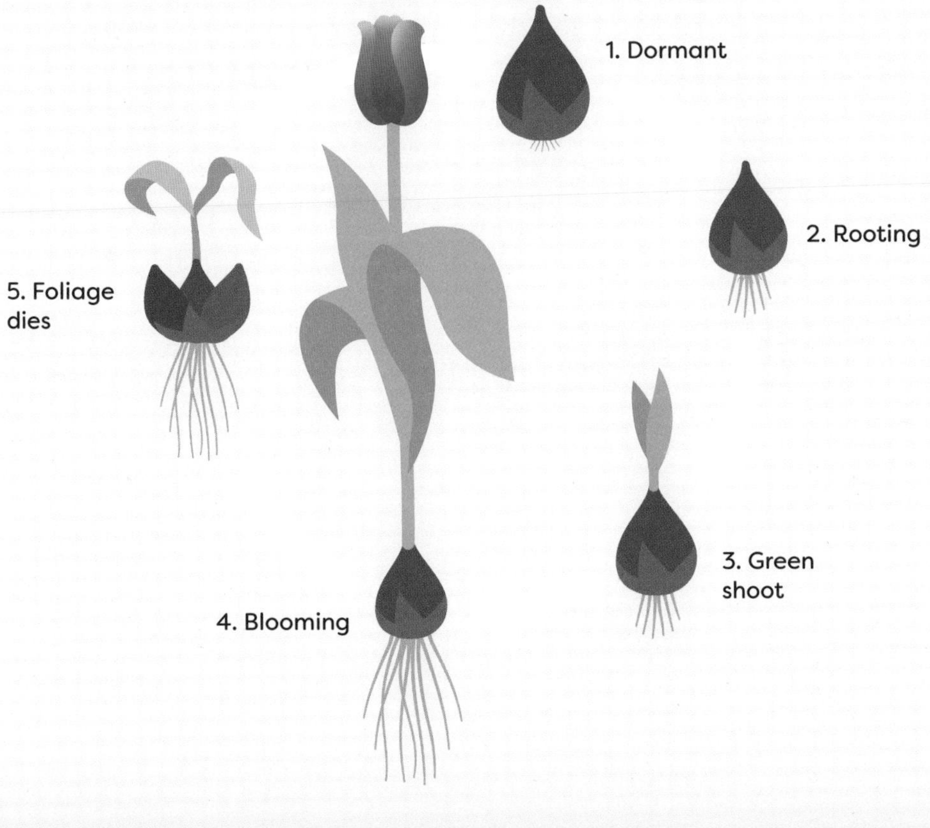

1. Dormant

2. Rooting

5. Foliage dies

3. Green shoot

4. Blooming

39

"Does Dickon know all about them?" Mary asked, as a new idea sprung up inside her.

"Our Dickon can make a flower grow out of a brick wall. Mother says he just whispers things out o' th' ground."

"Do bulbs live a long time if no one helps them?" Mary asked, anxious to know more.

"If you don't trouble 'em, most of 'em'll work away underground for a lifetime an' spread out an' have little 'uns," Martha explained.

"I wish the spring was here now," said Mary. "I want to see all the things that grow in England. I wish I had a little spade."

"Whatever does tha' want a spade for?" asked Martha, laughing. "Art tha' goin' to take to diggin'? I must tell mother that, too."

Mary looked at the fire thoughtfully. She must be careful to keep her secret. She wasn't doing any harm, but Mr. Craven would be angry if he found out and might change the lock on the door.

NEW GROWTH

Mary wants to plant new seeds to bring the secret garden to life.

What conditions might the seeds need to grow successfully? Turn to page 44 to watch some bean seeds germinate.

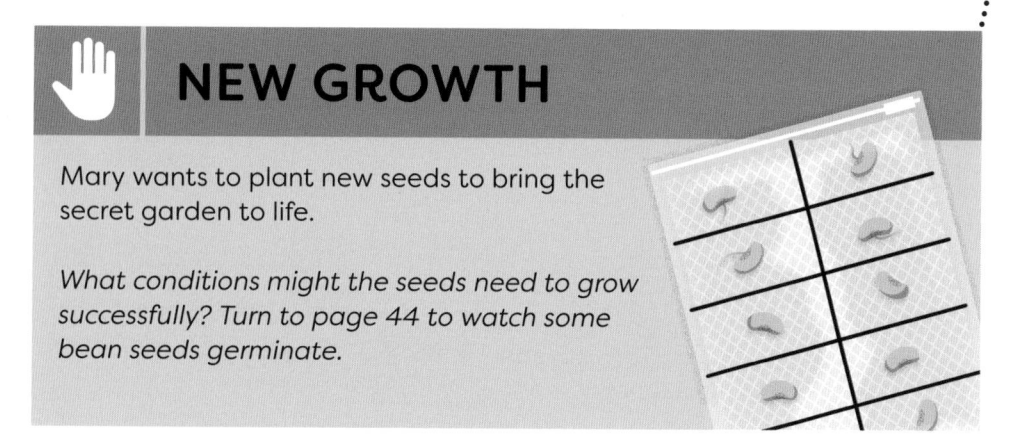

"Mrs. Medlock gives me a shilling from Mr. Craven every Saturday to spend. I thought if I had a spade, I might make a little garden, if I had some seeds."

Martha's face lit up. "If that wasn't one of th' things mother said!" she exclaimed. "In the shop at Thwaite they sell seeds and little garden sets. Does tha' know how to print letters?" she asked suddenly. "We could write to ask Dickon to buy them." Mary couldn't spell particularly well, but she wrote the words Martha dictated. So much excitement in one day!

That evening, just before Martha went downstairs for the tea tray, Mary asked a question. "Martha, has the scullery-maid had a toothache again today?"

"What makes thee ask that?" Martha replied with a little jump.

"Because when I walked down the corridor to see if you were coming, I heard that crying again, that's three times now. There isn't a wind today, so it couldn't have been the wind."

"Eh!" said Martha. "Tha' mustn't go walkin' about in corridors an' listenin'. Mr. Craven would be that angry, there's no knowin' what he'd do. My word! There's Mrs. Medlock's bell," and she ran out of the room.

"It's the strangest house anyone ever lived in," said Mary drowsily, as the fresh air, skipping, and digging got the better of her and she fell asleep.

BUILD A COMBINATION LOCK

To Mary's excitement, the buried key turns the lock in the old garden door. Try creating a lock of your own, but keep the combination a secret!

1

Ask an adult to help you cut a window in one side of the cardboard box, as shown.

YOU WILL NEED:

- small square cardboard box
- corrugated cardboard
- pencil and black felt-tip
- scissors
- glue gun
- sheet of printer-size paper
- wooden craft stick, with ½ inch (cut from one end

2

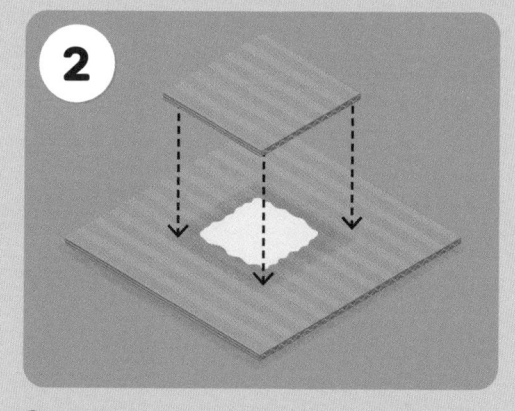

Cut out a square of corrugated cardboard, about ½ inch (1cm) bigger than your cut-out window. Then cut out a smaller square and glue together, as shown.

3

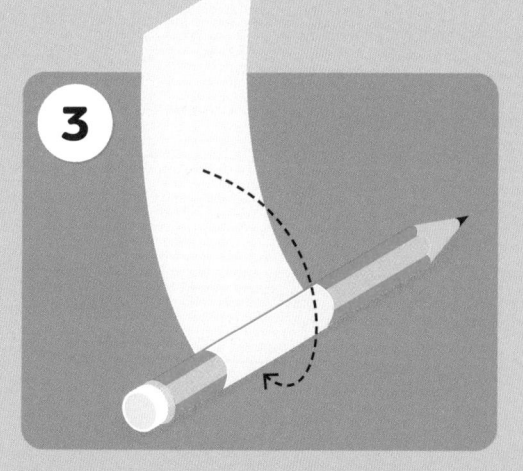

Cut a strip of printer paper, about 1.5 inches (4cm) wide, and wind it around your pencil. Cut your coiled paper so it's about ½ inch (1cm) wide, with straight edges.

4

Ask an adult to help you drill a hole in the center of your corrugated squares from step 2. Put your coiled paper in the hole. Cut a small circle of cardstock and mark numbers around the edge, as shown. Stick it to the front side of the coiled paper.

5

Now glue the wooden craft stick to the other side of the coiled paper, as shown. This is your combination lock.

6

Place your combination lock over the box window. Glue on a small paper hinge and draw an arrow above the circle. Turn the circle so the door stays shut. Write down the number at which the door opens. Keep this number a secret, and store some treasures!

WHY IT WORKS

The wooden craft stick acts as a lock which keeps the door closed and the coiled paper acts as a lever. When you turn the wheel, the craft stick turns too. There's a point at which the craft stick doesn't cover the door, so you can open it smoothly. Combination locks work in a similar way. When the right combination is used, the wheels and notches inside the lock line up perfectly so that it opens.

SEED GERMINATION

Mary wants the secret garden to come alive again and plans to plant new seeds. Try this simple germination activity to see how bean seeds start to grow.

1

Draw a 5x2 frame on the plastic bag with the black marker, as shown.

YOU WILL NEED:

- plastic zip-up bag
- black permanent marker
- paper towel
- bean seeds
- water spray

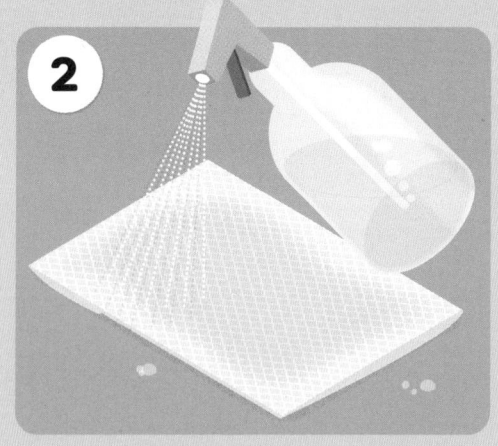

2

Fold the paper towel so it fits inside the plastic bag. Moisten the paper towel with the water spray.

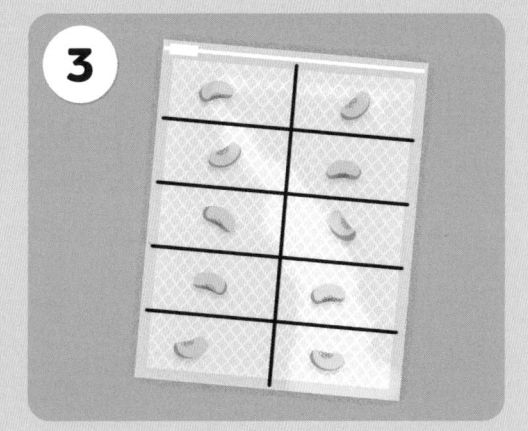

3

Place the paper towel inside the plastic bag, and place one seed into each "compartment," as shown.

4

Close the bag and place in a sunny spot near a window.

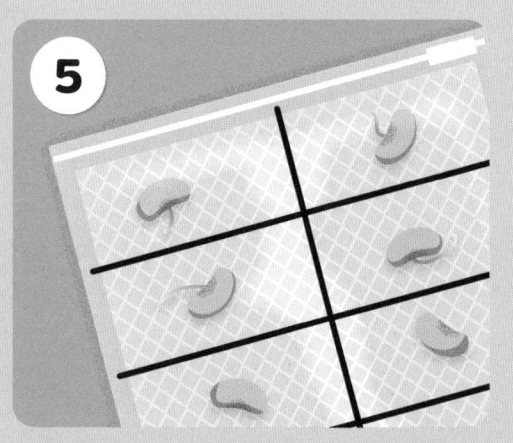

5

Watch your seeds over a few days. Which seeds start to grow a root and a shoot?

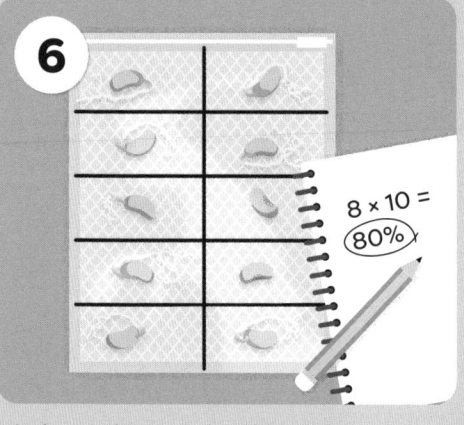

6

$8 \times 10 =$
80%

Work out the germination rate (percentage) of your bean seeds by multiplying the number of seeds that germinate by 10.

WHY IT WORKS

When seeds germinate, they begin to grow a root and a shoot. Some seeds fail to germinate because the conditions aren't quite right. Seeds need water, oxygen, and the correct temperature and light levels to grow. Knowing the "germination rate" of seeds can be useful to farmers. They can choose to plant more seeds so they still harvest the desired number of plants.

Chapter 4

Dickon

Mary found new green shoots every day. She wondered how long it would be before they were flowers.

"If you had a flower garden," Mary asked Ben Weatherstaff one morning, "what would you plant?"

"Bulbs an' sweet-smellin' things—but mostly roses."

"Oh, do you like roses! How can you tell whether they're dead or alive?" Mary asked.

He looked curiously at her eager face. "Why does tha' care so much about roses all of a sudden?" he demanded.

Mary was almost afraid to answer. "I-I want a garden of my own," she stammered. "There's nothing for me to do here."

She asked as many questions as she dared before she went off skipping again. There was a laurel-hedged walk which led to the woods, and she thought she'd see if there were any rabbits hopping about. At the gate, she heard a low, whistling sound. Mary caught her breath. A boy was sitting against a tree, playing a wooden pipe.

MUSICAL INSTRUMENTS

When you play a musical instrument, you make the air vibrate by blowing, plucking, or banging to make a sound. The way you play an instrument can change the frequency (the rate per second of a vibration) to give a different pitch. A low frequency gives a low pitch, and a high frequency gives a high pitch.

On a stringed instrument, thicker strings vibrate more slowly, so they have a lower sound. You can also use your fingers to make the strings shorter, to give them a higher pitch.

On a brass or wind instrument, changing the length of the pipe changes the pitch. On a trombone, for example, extending the slide makes the instrument longer and the sound lower. On a flute, for example, using the keys lengthens or shortens the distance the air travels.

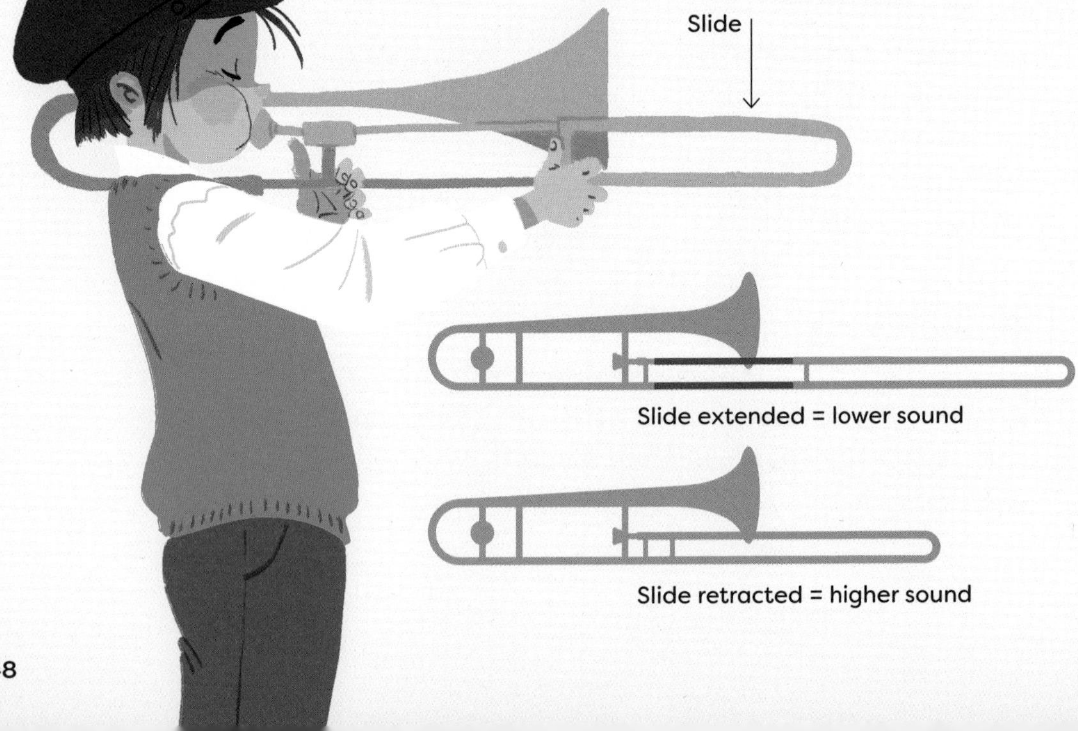

Slide

Slide extended = lower sound

Slide retracted = higher sound

A brown squirrel was clinging to the tree watching him, a pheasant was peeping out from a bush nearby, and two rabbits were sitting up and sniffing. It was as if they were all drawing near to watch him and listen to his music.

When he saw Mary, he held up his hand and spoke to her in a low voice. "Don't tha' move," he said. "It'd flight 'em."

The boy stopped playing and slowly rose from the ground. "I'm Dickon," he said with a wide smile. "I know tha'rt Miss Mary."

"Did you get Martha's letter?" she asked.

He nodded. "That's why I come. I've got th' garden tools as well as the seeds you wanted."

They sat down and looked through the seeds together, and as they did so Dickon stopped and turned his head quickly, his face lighting up. "Where's that robin as is callin' us?" he said.

"Is it really calling us?" she asked.

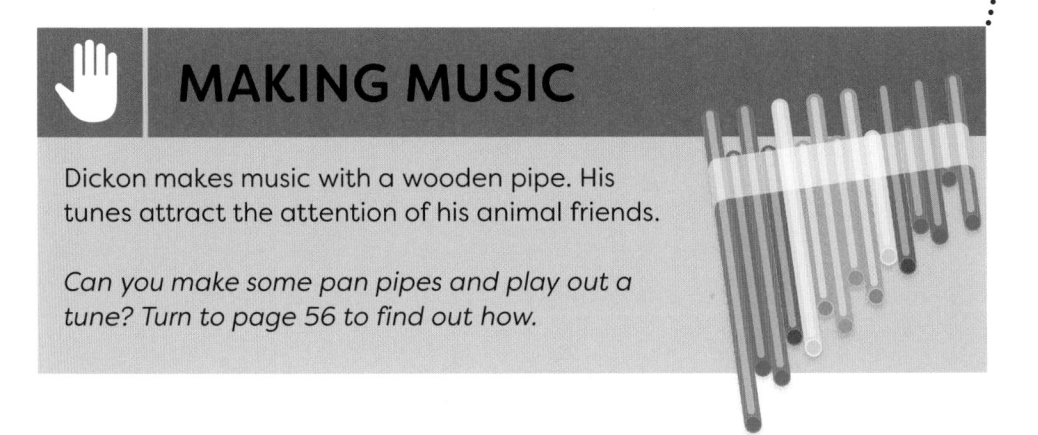

✋ MAKING MUSIC

Dickon makes music with a wooden pipe. His tunes attract the attention of his animal friends.

Can you make some pan pipes and play out a tune? Turn to page 56 to find out how.

"Aye," said Dickon, "he's callin' someone he's friends with. There he is in the bush. Whose is he?"

"He's Ben Weatherstaff's, but I think he knows me a little now," Mary replied.

"Aye, he knows thee," said Dickon. "An' he likes thee. He'll tell me all about thee in a minute."

Dickon moved slowly toward the bush and then made a sound almost like the robin's own twitter. The robin listened for a few seconds, and then answered as if he was replying.

"Aye, he's a friend o' yours," chuckled Dickon as he came back and began to talk about the flower seeds again. "Where is tha' garden?"

Mary didn't know what to say, so for a whole minute she said nothing. She'd never thought of this. She felt miserable.

"Tha's got a bit o' garden, hasn't tha?" Dickon said.

Mary turned her eyes toward him. "Could you keep a secret? I don't know what I'd do if anyone found out. I believe I should die!" She said the last words quite fiercely.

Dickon looked more puzzled than ever, but answered kindly, "I'm keepin' secrets all th' time," he said, "about foxes' cubs, an' birds' nests, an' wild things' holes. Aye, I can keep secrets for sure."

WHAT DO PLANTS NEED TO GROW?

Plants need five things to grow—sunlight, water, air, nutrients, and a healthy temperature.

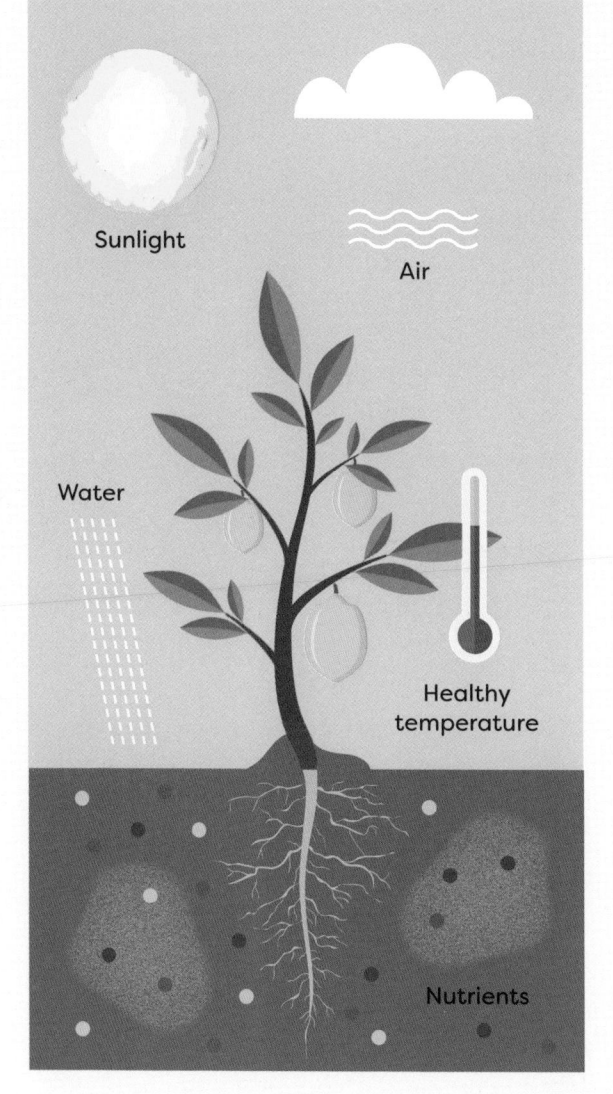

Sunlight

Air

Water

Healthy temperature

Nutrients

Sunlight gives a plant energy to grow and to make its own food. Water is vital to keep plant cells stiff, to make the plant's food, and to transport nutrients through the stems and leaves. Plants also use the carbon dioxide in air to make their food. Most plants take nutrients from the soil. Plants can die if conditions get too hot or too cold.

Some plants, such as cacti, have adapted to grow in hot deserts. Others, such as air plants, have adapted to grow without soil. Air plants grow high up in a rain forest canopy, for example. They have special scales on their leaves to get nutrients and moisture from the air.

"I've stolen a garden," she said very fast. "It isn't mine. It isn't anybody's. Nobody wants it. They're letting it die, all shut in by itself," she ended passionately, and she threw her arms over her face and burst out crying.

"Eh-h-h!" Dickon said, with wonder and sympathy. "Where is it?" he asked in a low voice.

Mary led him through the door behind the hanging ivy. "It's this," Mary said, waving her hand around defiantly. "It's a secret garden, and I'm the only one in the world who wants it to be alive."

Dickon looked around. "Eh!" he almost whispered. "It's just like a dream. I never thought I'd see this place."

"Did you know about it?" Mary whispered.

Dickon nodded. "Martha told me—we used to wonder what it was like."

"Will there be roses?" Mary whispered. "Can you tell? I thought perhaps they were all dead."

"Eh! No! Not all of 'em!" he answered. "Look here!"

He showed her how the most lifeless-looking branches had some green lower down. Dickon cut the dry, dead wood away and showed her how to stir the earth and let the air in.

"Tha's done a lot o' work already!" he said, looking around.

"Will you come again and help me?" Mary begged. "Oh please do come, Dickon!"

"I'll come every day if tha' wants me, rain or shine," he answered gladly. "It's a secret garden," he said, "but seems like someone besides th' robin must have been in it. There's been a bit o' prunin' done here an' there, later than ten year' ago."

Mary was startled and disappointed when she heard the big clock strike midday. "I shall have to go for lunch," she said mournfully.

Dickon had brought some lunch of his own. "I'll do some more before I head home."

"Whatever happens, you'll never tell?" Mary said.

Dickon smiled encouragingly. "Tha' art as safe as a missel thrush who's shown me her nest."

Mary's dinner was waiting on the table when she got in. "Tha's a bit late," Martha said. "Where has tha' been?"

"I've seen Dickon!" Mary said. She was afraid Martha might ask difficult questions, but she just asked about the gardening tools.

Mary ate her dinner as quickly as she could and was just about to run for her hat, when Martha stopped her. "Mr. Craven came back this mornin' and he wants to see you."

Mary turned pale. "Oh! Why? He didn't want to see me when I came."

"Mother passed him in Thwaite village. She said somethin' as put him in th' mind to see you. He's goin' abroad tomorrow for a long time. He mayn't come back till autumn or winter."

"When do you think he'll want to see—" She didn't finish the sentence because Mrs. Medlock walked in. "Your hair's rough," she said quickly. "Go and brush it. Martha, help her to slip on her best dress."

Mary's heart began to thump. She followed Mrs. Medlock down the corridors in silence. She was taken to a part of the house she'd not been in before. A man was sitting in an armchair by the fire. "This is Miss Mary, sir," Mrs. Medlock said.

"You can leave her here," the man said. He was not ugly. His face would have been handsome if he'd not been so miserable. He looked as if he didn't know what to do with her. "Do they take good care of you?" he asked. "You're very thin."

"I'm filling out these days," she replied. His black eyes seemed as if they scarcely saw her, as if they were seeing something else.

GROWING CONDITIONS

Mary wants to plant some seeds to help the secret garden come back to life.

What will Mary need for her plants to thrive? Turn to page 58 to find out which soil works best.

"I intended to send you a governess or a nurse, but I forgot," he said.

"Please," began Mary, "I'm too big for a nurse, and please don't make me have a governess yet."

"Mrs. Sowerby said you'd better get stronger before you had a governess. Play outdoors as much as you like. Is there anything you want? Do you want toys, books, dolls?"

"Might I have a bit of earth?" quavered Mary. "To plant seeds in, to make things grow, to see them come alive."

"You can have as much earth as you want," he said, and his dark eyes softened. "You remind me of someone else who loved the earth and things that grow. There! You must go now, I'm tired."

When Mary saw Martha, she couldn't contain her excitement. "I can have my garden!" she cried. "I'm not going to have a governess! He's really a nice man after all."

She ran straight to the garden, but it was empty—except for the robin who'd just settled on a rose bush watching her. Mary noticed a piece of paper attached to a thorn. It had a picture of a bird's nest and some roughly printed letters, "I will cum bak." When Mary showed Martha later, she said it was a missel thrush on her nest. Then Mary knew Dickon's picture was a message—that he'd keep her secret!

PROJECT

MAKE PAN PIPES

Dickon plays a wooden pipe to charm his animal friends. Create your own pan pipes to make some tunes of your own.

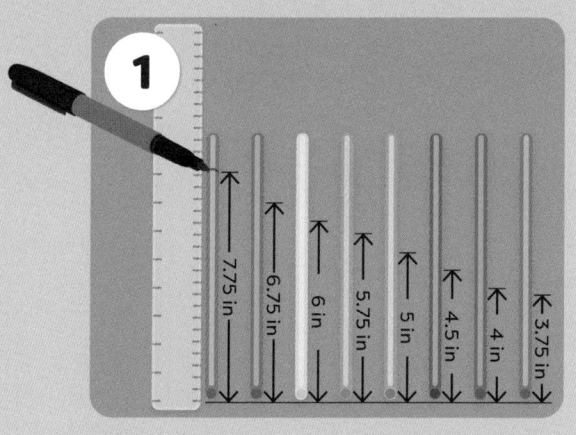

Use your ruler to measure the straws and mark with the marker pen at the following lengths: 7.75 in., 6.75 in., 6 in., 5.75 in., 5 in., 4.5 in., 4 in., 3.75 in.

YOU WILL NEED:

- 8 straws
- ruler
- scissors
- black permanent marker
- masking tape
- wooden craft stick (optional)

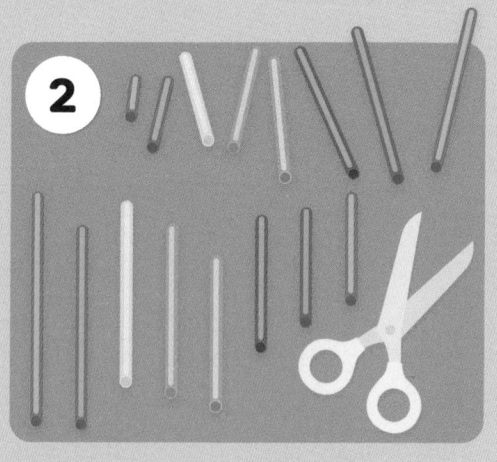

Cut your straws to the marked lengths and keep the spare ends.

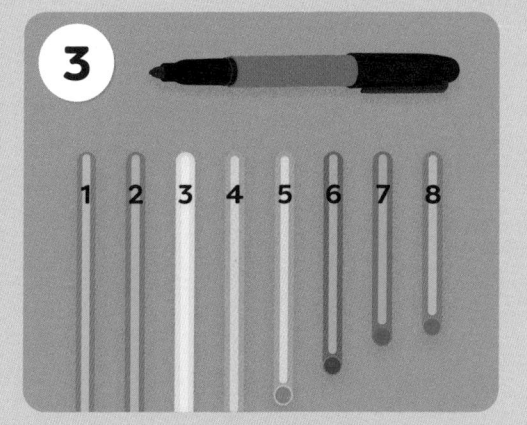

Number each straw with the marker, with 1 the longest and 8 the shortest.

Lay your straws on a flat surface and place the spare ends between each straw as shown. This will make it easier to blow each straw in turn. Tape the straws together. You can use a wooden craft stick as a support if needed.

Gently blow across the top of your straws. What do you notice about the sound of straw 1 and straw 8?

Now you can create some simple tunes. Try these two for starters!

333 333 35123

321 321 5443 5443

WHY IT WORKS

When you blow on your pan pipes, the air inside the straws vibrates. Sounds are higher or lower in pitch, depending on the frequency (the rate per second of a vibration). A long straw has a low frequency (low pitch) and a short straw has a high frequency (high pitch). You should find that straws 1 and 8 sound similar (they're an octave apart). Every time the pitch goes up one octave, the frequency doubles.

COMPARE SOIL TYPES

Mary asks Mr. Craven for a bit of earth so she can plant seeds and help them to grow. Use this experiment to find out which soil is best for growing seeds.

1

Fill the jam jars half full with the following soils: garden soil; sand; potting soil; half sand, half potting soil. Use the marker to label each jar with the soil type it contains.

YOU WILL NEED:

- 4 jam jars
- Black permanent marker
- pencil
- garden soil
- sand
- potting soil (from a garden center)
- packet of seeds
- water and measuring cup

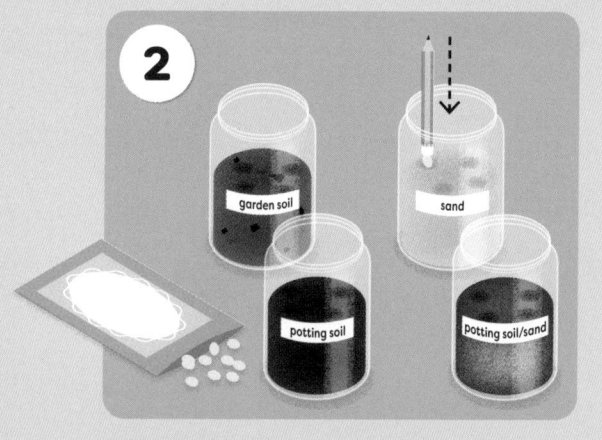

2

Plant four seeds in each jar. You can push the seeds gently into the soil with a pencil.

3

Water each jar with half a cup of water.

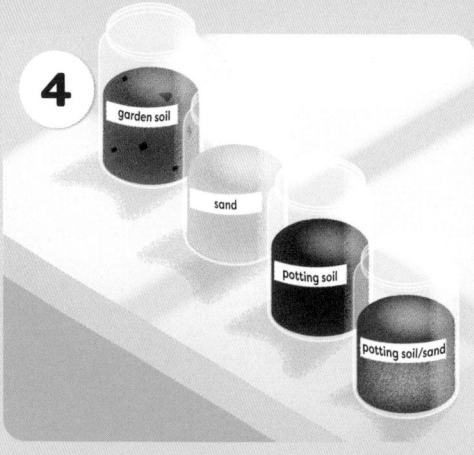

4

Place your jars on a sunny windowsill.

5

Leave for a week and record any growth that appears. Draw and describe what you see.

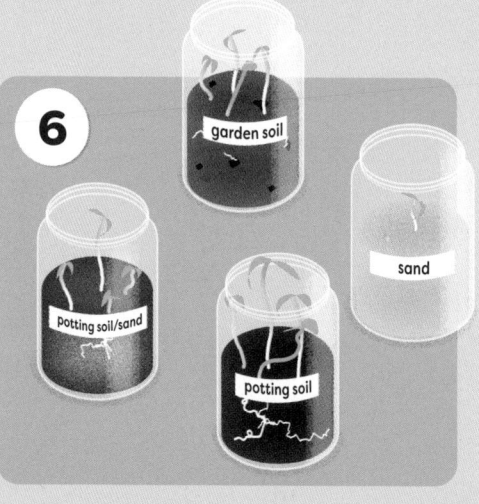

6

Compare the growth again after two weeks. Which soils gave the most growth? Which gave the least?

WHY IT WORKS

Different soils have different levels of nutrients. Potting soil is specially blended to help plants to thrive. It also gives the roots enough space to grow. Garden soil can become waterlogged and too compact for the roots to spread out. Some seeds grow surprisingly well in sand. Seeds are already packed with nutrients, so some soils work well when a seed germinates but are less good as the plant continues to grow.

Chapter 5

Master Colin

That night, Mary had been woken by the sound of rain beating against her window and the wind howling when something startled her. "It isn't the wind now," she thought. "It's that crying again."

She took her candle and walked softly down the long, dark corridor, gently pushing the door beneath the tapestry. She could see a glimmer of light through a door ahead. The crying was coming from that room!

She pushed the door gently. A fire was glowing in the hearth and a boy was lying on a four-poster bed, crying fretfully. He had a sharp, delicate face the color of ivory and eyes too big for his face, with heavy locks that tumbled over his forehead. He looked like he'd been ill, but was crying more from frustration and tiredness, than pain.

As Mary crept across the room, her candle attracted his attention. He turned his head and stared. "Are you a ghost?" he whispered.

"No, are you?" Mary whispered back.

"I'm Colin. Colin Craven. Who are you?"

"I'm Mary Lennox. Mr. Craven is my uncle."

"He's my father," said the boy.

"Your father!" gasped Mary. "No one told me he had a son! Did no one tell you I'd come to live here? I couldn't sleep. Why were you crying?"

"Because I couldn't sleep either and my head ached. They didn't tell me because I'd be afraid you'd see me looking so ill. The servants aren't allowed to speak of me. If I live, I may be a hunchback, but I shan't live. My mother died when I was born, and it makes my father wretched to look at me."

"Do you want me to go away?" Mary asked.

"No," he said, "sit down and talk. I want to hear about you." Mary settled herself and told him her story.

"How old are you?" he asked. "Ten," Mary replied, "and so are you." "How do you know?" he demanded.

"Because when you were born the garden door was locked and the key was buried, ten years ago."

"What garden door?" he exclaimed.

REST AND RECUPERATION

Colin's room is full of antique furniture, and he rests and sleeps in a four-poster bed.

Can you make a miniature four-poster bed of your own? Turn to page 70 for some tips.

"The garden Mr. Craven hates," said Mary nervously. "No one knows where he buried the key and no one's been allowed to go in for ten years."

Mary tried to answer carefully, but it was too late. Colin asked question after question. Had she never looked for the door? Had she asked the gardeners?

"I think they've been told not to answer questions," she said.

"I would make them," said Colin. "Everyone's obliged to please me."

Mary didn't realize she'd been spoiled in India, but she could see quite plainly that Colin thought the whole world belonged to him.

"Why do you think you'll die?" Mary asked, partly from curiosity and partly to distract him from the garden.

"I've heard people say it all my life. My doctor is my father's cousin. He'll have Misselthwaite if my father and I die. I should think he wouldn't want me to live. Let us talk about something else. I want to see that garden. I'm going to make them open the door."

Mary clutched her hands together. "Oh, don't do that!" she cried, "It'll never be a secret again. If we find the door, we could shut it behind us and call it our own garden." Mary began to describe to Colin what the garden *might* be like, and about a friendly robin that *might* live there.

PULLEYS

Pulleys are simple machines. They use one or more wheels and a rope to make lifting or pulling easier. The more wheels a pulley system has, the easier it is to lift a load.

If you have a pulley with one wheel, you pull down on the rope to lift the weight up. However, you still need to use the same force and pull the rope the same distance to raise the load.

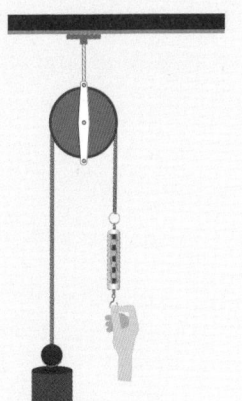

If you have two wheels, you will find you need to pull with half the force! However, you will need to pull the rope twice the distance, to raise the load.

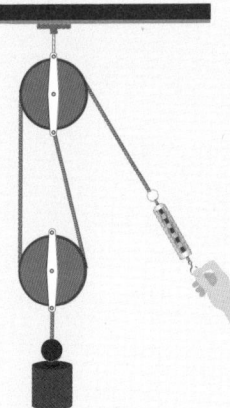

Pull down 1 feet to lift weight 1 feet

Pull down 2 feet to lift weight 1 feet

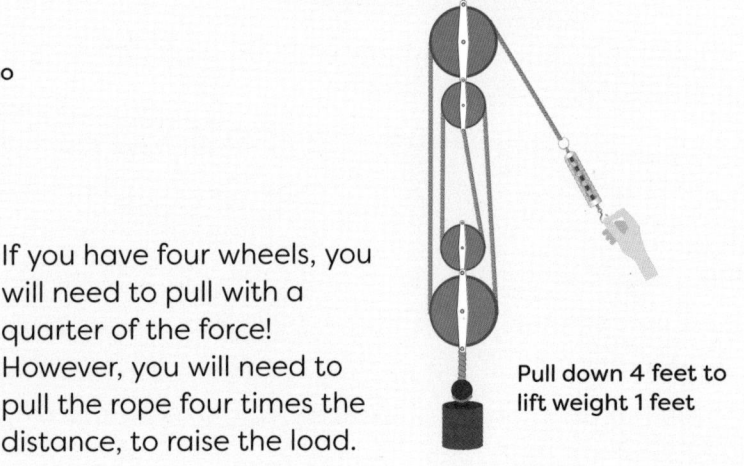

If you have four wheels, you will need to pull with a quarter of the force! However, you will need to pull the rope four times the distance, to raise the load.

Pull down 4 feet to lift weight 1 feet

"What a lot of things you know," Colin said. "If you stay in a room, you never see things." He was quiet for a moment and then he said, "Can you pull the cord hanging from that silk curtain over the mantelpiece?"

It uncovered a picture of a girl smiling. Her hair was tied with a blue ribbon and her lovely eyes were just like Colin's unhappy ones, with black lashes all around them.

"She's my mother," said Colin complainingly. "I don't see why she died. Sometimes I hate her for doing it. If she'd lived, I believe I should not always have been ill. And my father would not have hated to look at me. Draw the curtain again. She smiles too much when I'm miserable."

They were silent for a moment. "What would Mrs. Medlock do if she found out I'd been here?" Mary asked.

"She would do as I told her," he said. "I wanted you to come here. I'm glad you came."

OPEN AND CLOSED

The portrait of Colin's mother is behind a pulley curtain. Colin likes to keep the curtain closed most of the time.

Can you make a pulley curtain to reveal a picture of your own? Turn to page 72 to find out how.

"So am I," Mary said. "I will come as often as I can."

"I think you shall be a secret, too," said Colin. "I won't tell them until they find out. The nurse makes Martha attend to me when she goes out. Martha can tell you when to come."

Then Mary understood Martha's troubled look about the crying.

"I've been here a long time," said Mary. "Your eyes look sleepy."

"I wish I could go to sleep before you leave," he said shyly.

"Shut your eyes," said Mary, and she chanted and stroked his head like her nanny used to do, before she crept away without a sound.

The next day was wet—there could be no going outdoors. Mary asked Martha to come when she'd finished her chores. "I've found out what the crying was," Mary said. "It was Colin. I found him."

Martha gazed at her with startled eyes. "Eh! Miss Mary! Tha' shouldn't have done it! Tha'll get me in trouble. I never told thee nothin' about him. I'll lose my place!"

"You won't," said Mary gently. "He wants me to talk to him, and you're to tell me when to go. You can't lose your place if you're doing what he wants. What's the matter with him?"

"Nobody knows for sure," said Martha. "Mr. Craven went off his head when he was born because Mrs. Craven died. He wouldn't set eyes on th' baby. He just raved and said it'd be another hunchback like him, and it'd better die."

"Is Colin a hunchback?" Mary asked. "He didn't look like one."

"He isn't yet," said Martha. "But he didn't have a good start. They was afraid his back was weak and he's had terrible coughs an' colds that's nearly killed him."

"I wonder if it'd do him good to go outside and watch things grow."

Just then a bell rang. Martha came back ten minutes later with a puzzled expression on her face. "He's sent for you. Remember not to tell anyone."

When Mary mentioned how worried Martha was, Colin ordered her to come to his room. "If I order you to bring Miss Mary to me, how can Medlock send you away if she finds out? I'll send *her* away if she dares say a word."

When Martha closed the door, Mary gave Colin a hard stare. "Why are you looking at me like that?" he said.

"The way you spoke to Martha reminded me of a Rajah in India. Everybody had to follow his orders. I was also thinking how different you are from Dickon."

"Who's Dickon?" Colin asked.

"He's Martha's brother. He's not like anyone else in the world. He can charm foxes and squirrels and birds. He plays on his pipe and they listen. I believe Dickon would make you feel better. He never talks about dead things or things that are ill. And he laughs such a big laugh."

As she talked about Dickon and his family, they both began to laugh. "Do you know there's one thing we've never thought of," he said. "We're cousins!" Which made them laugh even more, just as Dr. Craven and Mrs. Medlock walked in.

"What is this?" said Dr. Craven, frowning.

"This is my cousin, Mary Lennox. I asked her to come and talk to me. She must come whenever I send for her."

Dr. Craven turned as if to reprimand Mrs. Medlock. "Oh, sir," she panted. "I don't know how it's happened."

"Nobody told her anything," Colin explained. "She heard me crying and found me herself. I'm glad she came."

Dr. Craven didn't stay very long. He said a few words of warning to Colin—he must not forget that he was easily tired.

"I *want* to forget it," Colin cried out. "She makes me forget it. That's why I want her."

"Now," said Colin, turning to Mary. "Tell me about the Rajahs."

RAJAHS

Rajah is a term used to describe a monarch or princely ruler in India and parts of Southeast Asia. For hundreds of years, wealthy Rajahs controlled parts of India and ruled over vast areas of land from their splendid palaces.

The term maharaja means "great king." This word was used for particularly important rulers such as emperors, although many rajahs claimed to be a maharaja. The wife of a rajah was called a rani and the wife of a maharaja was called a maharani.

The British used the term Raj to describe their rule over India between 1858 and 1947. During this time, the Rajahs still retained some parts of India and were indirectly controlled by the British. They lost their power when the country gained independence in 1947, but still retain some influence in their regional areas.

MAKE A FOUR-POSTER BED

Colin spends many hours in his four-poster bed. Try creating your own miniature bed with a bundle of wooden craft sticks!

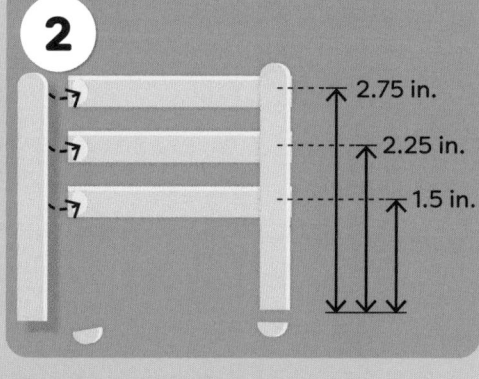

1

Cut the ends off five wooden craft sticks so they're all the same length, with straight edges as shown.

YOU WILL NEED:

- 27 wooden craft sticks
- strong scissors
- ruler
- pencil
- glue gun
- scrap material

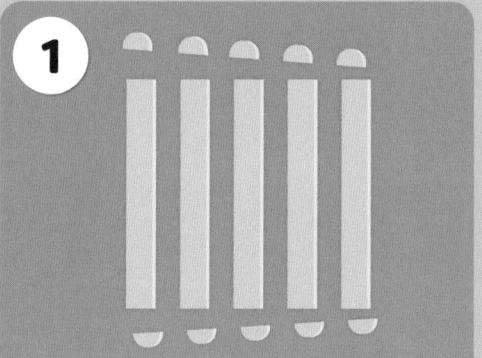

2

2.75 in.
2.25 in.
1.5 in.

Cut one end from two more craft sticks. Then measure and mark along the sides at 1.5 in., 2.25 in., and 2.75 in. Glue three of the slats from step 1 to these craft sticks as shown. This is your bed head.

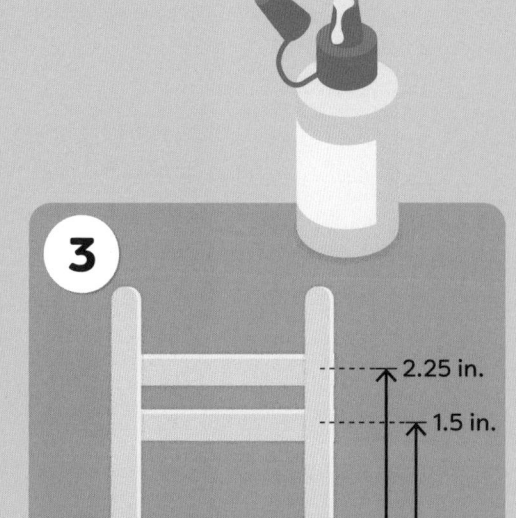

3

2.25 in.
1.5 in.

Cut one end from two more craft sticks. Measure and mark their sides at 1.5 in. and 2.25 in. Glue the last two slats from step 1 to these sticks as shown. This is the foot of your bed.

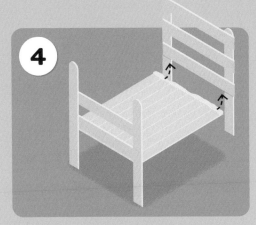

4

Cut both ends off fourteen more craft sticks. Glue eight of these to the bottom of your bed head, as shown. Then glue the foot of the bed to the other end. This is the base of your bed.

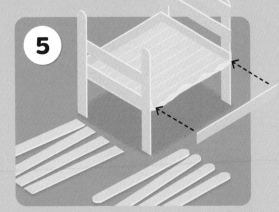

5

Glue two more of these craft sticks to the base of your bed as shown. These are the sides of your bed. In total, you should now have four of these craft sticks plus four uncut craft sticks left over to use in step 6.

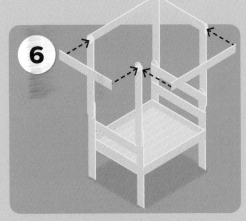

6

Glue the four uncut craft sticks to the head and foot of the bed as shown. These are the bed posts. Finally, glue the remaining four sticks from step 5 to the top of the bed posts. You could drape some material around the edge for the full effect!

WHY IT WORKS

Years ago, wealthy families often had four-poster beds. With no central heating in their big, drafty houses, four-poster beds were designed with thick curtains to keep out cold drafts. The curtains also provided privacy if a servant was sleeping in the same room, for example.

MAKE A PULLEY CURTAIN

The portrait of Colin's mother is behind a closed curtain. Make this pulley curtain to reveal artwork of your own.

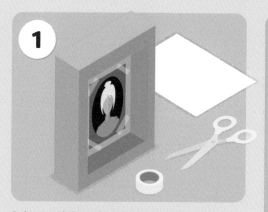

1

Ask an adult to help you cut a window from the cardboard box, leaving a 2-inch (5cm) rim around the edges. This will be your picture frame. Tape a picture to the inside.

YOU WILL NEED:

- scissors • tape
- scrap material • marker
- nylon string • 3 plastic bobbins
- 5 long butterfly clips
- needle and thread
- small cardboard box (about 12 inches or 30cm length)
- magazine picture or your own
- steel PVC-coated lanyard loop (about 8 inches or 20cm)
- stopwatch

2

Cut a piece of material the size of your box side, and cut in half. Wrap the top edge of each piece around the lanyard loop and stitch a hem to hold them in place so the fabric moves freely.

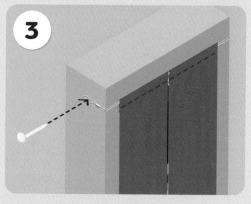

3

Ask an adult to help you attach the lanyard loop to the front of your box tightly with butterfly clips, so the fabric sits over the cut-out picture frame.

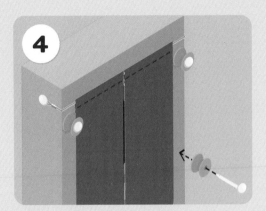

4

Ask an adult to help you attach the bobbins to the cardboard box with butterfly clips, as shown.

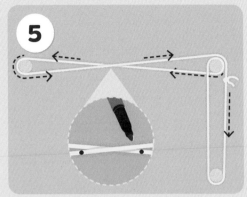

5

Thread the nylon string through the bobbins, as shown, and secure the loop tightly. Notice how the string loops around the top right bobbin. This is your pulley. Make a mark on the left and right of the pulley in the positions shown.

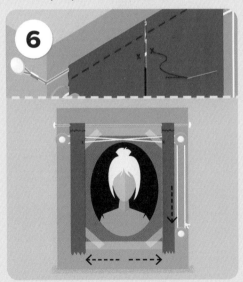

6

Ask an adult to help you sew the edge of the left curtain to the left mark on the pulley and the right curtain to the right mark. Pull the string of your vertical pulley and then pull in the opposite direction. What happens? Time how long it takes to open or close the curtains fully.

WHY IT WORKS

As you pull the string on the vertical pulley, the curtains should separate in the middle and bunch up to each side. If you pull the string on the vertical pulley the other way, the curtains should move back to the middle again. Nylon string works best because it creates less friction, making for a smooth mechanism. You can use the stopwatch to time the opening and closing. You could use a short piece of music, for example, for your final reveal!

Chapter 6

A Tantrum

With another week of rain, there was no chance of going outside. Mary spent hours with Colin. She wondered if he could keep the garden a secret, or how they could take him there unseen.

When the sky turned blue again, Mary woke early. She went straight to the garden, where Dickon was already hard at work. A little red animal with a bushy tail sat by him and a crow settled quietly on his shoulder. "This is th' little fox cub," he said. "It's named Captain. An' this here's Soot."

They found so many wonders in the garden that day. As they rested by a tree, watching quietly as the robin darted about building a nest, Mary shared her news. "Do you know about Colin?"

"What does tha' know about him?"

"I've seen him. I've talked to him every day. He says I'm making him forget about being ill and dying," Mary explained.

Dickon looked relieved. "I'm glad o' that," he exclaimed. "I knowed I must say nothin'."

"Do you think Mr. Craven wants him to die?" whispered Mary.

WHY DOES IT RAIN ON THE MOOR?

The water cycle is the continuous movement of water around Earth as a liquid, solid, or gas. Water is found as a solid in glaciers, for example, and as a gas in water vapor.

Heat from the Sun causes the water in streams, lakes, rivers, and oceans to evaporate into water vapor. As this warm gas rises, it cools and condenses into a liquid again, forming clouds. As more water condenses, the clouds become heavy and full.

Gravity causes the water to fall back to Earth as rain, sleet, or snow, and the cycle begins again.

Areas of moorland usually have a lot of rain. This is because they are areas of higher ground where temperatures are lower. Water vapor condenses more quickly in these regions, producing a wetter climate.

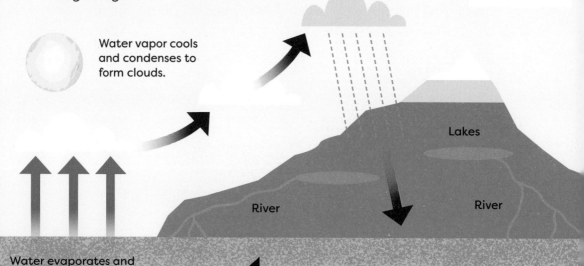

Rain falls back to ground.

Water vapor cools and condenses to form clouds.

Lakes

River

River

Water evaporates and rises over high land.

"No, but he wishes he'd never been born. Mother says that's th' worst thing for a child. He's also afraid he'll find he's growed a hunchback."

"Colin's so afraid of it himself that he won't sit up," Mary said.

"Eh! He oughtn't to lie there thinkin' things like that," said Dickon. "If Colin was out here, he wouldn't be watchin' for lumps to grow."

"I've been thinking the same," Mary said. "And if he wants us to take him out, no one dare disobey him."

They found a great deal to do that morning and Mary was late back for lunch. "Tell Colin I can't come yet," she said to Martha. "Dickon's waiting for me in the garden." And with that she ran off.

The afternoon was even busier than the morning. "It'll be fine tomorrow," said Dickon. "I'll be at work by sunrise."

"So will I!" Mary agreed and ran quickly back to the house. But when she got to her room, Martha had a worried face.

 ## RAINY DAYS

There is a lot of rain on the moor because the ground is so high. Mary can only visit the garden when the weather is fine.

Can you create a rain cloud of your own?
Turn to page 84 to find out how.

"Eh!" said Martha. "I wish tha'd gone. He was nigh goin' into one o' his tantrums. There's been a nice to do all afternoon to keep him quiet. He watched the clock all th' time."

Mary's lips pinched themselves together. She saw no reason why an ill-tempered boy should interfere with the thing she liked best.

He was lying flat on his back in bed and did not turn his head toward her when she came in. Mary marched up to him with her stiff manner.

"Why didn't you get up?" she said.

"I did when I thought you were coming," he answered. "I made them put me back to bed this afternoon. Why didn't you come?"

"I was working in the garden with Dickon," Mary said.

Colin frowned. "I won't let that boy come here if you go and stay with him instead of talking to me."

Mary felt furious. "If you send Dickon away, I'll never come into this room again!"

"I'll make you," said Colin. "They shall drag you in."

"Shall they, Mr. Rajah!" said Mary fiercely. "They may drag me in, but they can't make me talk. I'll sit and clench my teeth and never tell you a thing."

"You're a selfish girl!" Colin cried.

"You're the most selfish boy I ever met."

Colin had never had a fight with anyone like himself before. He was beginning to feel sorry for himself.

"I'm not as selfish as you, because I'm always ill, and I'm sure there's a lump growing on my back," he said. "And I'm going to die."

"You're not!" said Mary unsympathetically. "You just say that to make people worry. I believe you're proud of it."

Colin sat up and threw his pillow. "Get out of my room!" he shouted.

"I'm going," she said. "And I won't come back! I was going to tell you about the garden," she said. "Now I won't tell you a thing!"

Mary was cross and disappointed but not at all sorry for Colin. When she got back, Martha's face was full of curiosity. "Mr. Craven sent this for you," said Martha.

There was a wooden box full of neat packages—with several beautiful books inside, two about gardens, a few games, and a beautiful writing-case with a gold pen and inkstand. Everything was so nice that the anger Mary felt began to subside. "I will write a letter to tell him I'm much obliged," she said.

Mary had been sorry for Colin when he'd told her that most of his "tantrums" grew out of his hysterical hidden fear. "I said I'd never go back again, but perhaps I will in the morning," she thought.

In the middle of the night, she was woken by the dreadful sound of someone crying and screaming. Doors were banging and there were hurrying feet in the corridors.

"It's Colin," she thought. "He's having one of those tantrums the nurse called hysterics." She put her hands over her ears. "I can't bear it."

Suddenly she felt as if she'd fly into a tantrum herself and frighten him as he was frightening her. She was not used to anyone's temper but her own. She heard feet running down the corridor and the nurse came in. "He'll do himself harm," she said. "No one can do anything with him. You come and try, like a good child."

Mary flew along the corridor and the nearer she got, the more her temper grew. She threw the door open with her hand and ran across to the four-poster bed.

"You stop! I hate you! Everyone hates you! I wish they'd let you scream yourself to death! You *will* scream yourself to death in a minute!"

Colin was lying on his face, beating his pillow with his hands when the shock of Mary's words made him stop. His face looked dreadful—white, red, and swollen, and he was gasping and choking.

"If you scream," she said. "I'll scream too—and I'll frighten you!"

The scream which had been coming almost choked him. The tears were streaming down his face, and he shook all over. "I can't stop!" he gasped and sobbed. "I can't!"

"You can!" shouted Mary. "Half that ails you is hysterics and temper!" and she stamped her foot with these words.

"I felt the lump!" choked Colin. "I knew I would. I'm going to die."

"You didn't feel a lump!" Mary said fiercely. "There's nothing the matter with your back—turn over and let me look!"

It was a poor thin back—every bone could be counted. Mary looked up and down. "There's not a single lump!" she said at last, "except backbone lumps, and you can only feel them because you're so thin."

"I didn't know," said the nurse, "that he thought he had a lump on his spine. His back is weak because he won't try to sit up. I could have told him there was no lump there."

Colin turned on his face again and lay still for a minute. His long-drawn breaths were the only sound as his sobs died down. He put out his hand toward Mary, which she held, as she wanted to be friends.

"I'll go outside with you, Mary," he said. "If Dickon will push my chair. I do so want to see Dickon and his animals."

When the nurse had left them, Colin couldn't help but ask, "Have you found the way in?"

"I think I have," she answered. "Go to sleep and I'll tell you tomorrow."

"Oh, Mary! Could you tell me a little about what you imagine the garden looks like?" She talked of the flowers working their way out of the dark soil, and the uncurling leaves, and the robin building a nest. And with that, Colin was asleep.

COZY HOME

Mary and Dickon watch the robin gathering twigs and leaves to make a nest for his family.

Can you make a bird's nest too from some simple materials? Turn to page 86 for some guidance.

HOW DO BIRDS MAKE NESTS?

Nests provide a safe and warm place for birds to lay their eggs and raise their young. Birds use their beaks to gather twigs and stems and to weave them together.

Birds also use mud or their own saliva as a type of glue and gather moss, bark, and feathers to line the nest. Sometimes, birds use sticky spider webs as a type of foundation.

Cup nests are circular structures made of twigs and moss, while adherent nests are full of mud and often built against the side of trees or buildings. Some birds, such as owls, "rent" the nests of other birds or use existing tree hollows. Some birds don't make nests at all—they simply create crevices in the ground as a form of protection.

Adherent nest

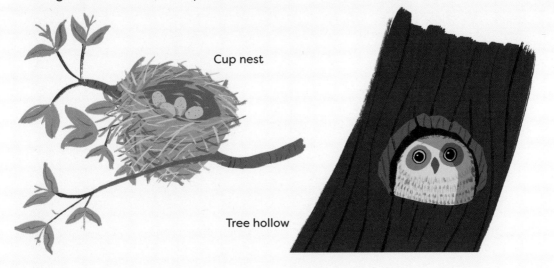

Cup nest

Tree hollow

83

MAKE A RAIN CLOUD

There are days when it's so rainy that Mary can't go out. Try making a rain cloud of your own.

1

Fill one jar three-quarters full with cool water.

YOU WILL NEED:

- two open jars (or glasses)
- water
- blue food coloring
- shaving foam
- plastic pipette

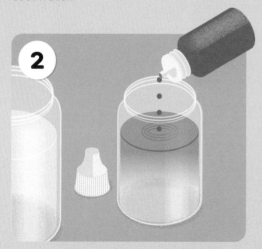

2

Add a few drops of food coloring to some water in the other jar.

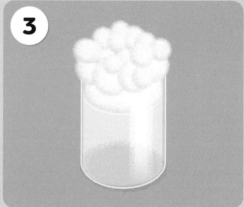

3

Squirt shaving foam on top of the water in the first jar, to make a "fluffy cloud."

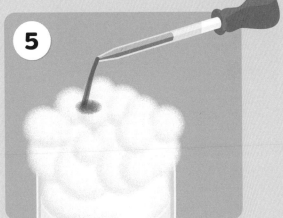

Using the pipette, take some colored water from the second jar.

Squirt the coloured water onto the "cloud."

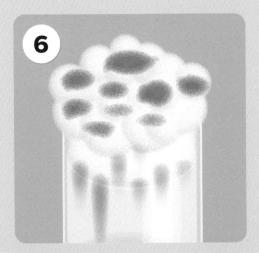

WHY IT WORKS

Repeat for a minute or two, until you see some blue "rain" seeping through the cloud.

When you squirt water onto the "cloud," it gets heavier and heavier. Eventually, the drops of water make their way through the cloud to the water beneath. In a similar way, rain clouds get heavier when more and more water vapor in the air condenses. The water droplets grow bigger and gravity pulls the water droplets back to Earth as rain, sleet, or snow.

BUILD A BIRD'S NEST

The robin is busy gathering materials for a nest. Try building your own bird's nest from outdoor materials.

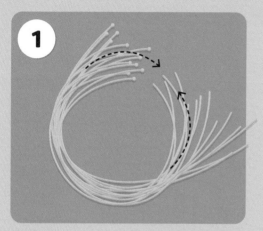

1

Take a handful of plant stems, such as straw, grass, or vines, and bend them into a loop.

YOU WILL NEED:

- long plant stems (such as straw, grass, or vines)
- small twigs, leaves, bark, moss
- string • scissors

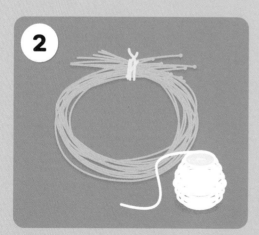

2

Add more stems to create a full circle. Tie the ends in place with the string.

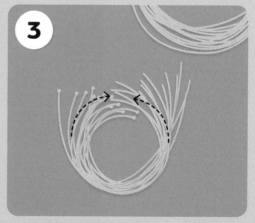

3

Take a smaller handful of stems and shape them into a smaller loop/circle.

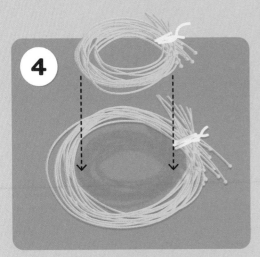

Put the smaller loop inside the larger loop and push downward. Tie the loops together with string if needed.

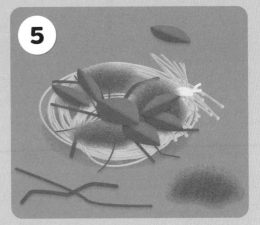

Use small twigs, leaves, bark, or moss to line the bottom of your nest.

You could add some eggs to your nest for the finished effect!

WHY IT WORKS

Birds use their beaks to weave twigs and stems together to create a firm structure for their nests. They also use mud and their own saliva as a type of glue. The circular shape of the bird's nest gives it strength and allows the eggs to stay close together while the parent bird sits on them to keep them warm.

Chapter 7

Spring has Sprung

Mary did not wake early the next morning because she was exhausted. When Martha brought her breakfast, she said that Colin wished to see her as soon as possible. He was in bed, his face was pitifully white, and there were dark circles around his eyes.

"I'm glad you came," he said. "I ache all over because I'm so tired. Are you going somewhere?"

"I'm going to see Dickon, but I'll come back. It's something about the secret garden."

A little color came back into his face. "Oh, I dreamed of it last night! It was beautiful. I'll lie and think of it until you come back."

When she got to the garden, Mary told Dickon all about the night's events. "Eh! we mun get him out here an' we munnot lose no time about it."

The garden was so beautiful it was hard to leave. The fox and the crow were there again as well as two tame squirrels—Nut and Shell. But Mary went back to the house to see Colin. She told him all about Dickon and his entourage of animals.

"I shouldn't mind Dickon looking at me," Colin said thoughtfully. "I want to see him."

"I'm glad you said that," Mary answered, "because Dickon said he'll come to see you tomorrow morning, and he'll bring his creatures."

Colin cried out in delight.

"But that's not all," Mary went on. "There's a door into the garden. I found it. It's under the ivy on the wall."

"Oh Mary!" Colin cried out with a sob. "Shall I *live* to see it?"

"Of course you'll see it!" snapped Mary indignantly. "Don't be silly!" And with that they began laughing and Colin's aches were forgotten.

Dr. Craven had been sent for that morning. "How is he?" he asked Mrs. Medlock rather irritably when he arrived.

"Well, sir," she replied, "you'll scarcely believe your eyes. That plain sour-faced child has bewitched him. She flew at him like a little cat last night and ordered him to stop screaming. Just come up and see."

The scene was indeed astonishing. Colin was sitting up quite straight on the sofa looking at a book and talking to the girl.

"I'm sorry to hear you were ill last night, my boy," Dr. Craven said.

"I'm better now," Colin answered. "I'm going out in my chair in a day or two if it's fine. I want some fresh air."

WIND AND WEATHER

Wind is the movement of air from areas of high pressure to areas of low pressure. The wind moves fastest when the difference between these two is the greatest.

In areas of high pressure, cool air is descending. This causes light winds and clear skies because clouds are unable to form. In areas of low pressure, warm air is rising. The water vapor in this air cools and condenses to form clouds. That's why areas of high pressure are associated with dry weather, while areas of low pressure are associated with cloudy, wet, and windy weather.

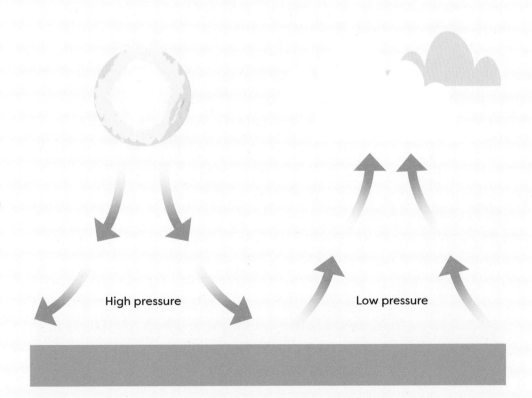

High pressure

Low pressure

Dr. Craven felt his pulse and looked at him curiously. "It must be a very fine day, and you must be very careful not to tire yourself. I thought you didn't like fresh air?"

"I don't when I'm by myself," Colin replied, "but my cousin is going with me. And a very strong boy I know will push my carriage."

"He must be a strong and steady boy," Dr. Craven said, "and I must know something about him."

"It's Dickon," Mary spoke up, and Dr. Craven's face relaxed into a smile. "Oh, you'll be safe enough," he said. "He's as strong as a pony!"

"It's certainly a new state of affairs," Dr. Craven said to Mrs. Medlock as he left. "And there's no denying it's better than the old one."

That night, Colin slept well and in the morning his mind was buzzing with the plans he and Mary had made. He'd not been awake for more than ten minutes when Mary ran through the door. "It's so beautiful," she said, a little breathless. "It's come, the Spring! Dickon says so!"

"Has it?" cried Colin. "Open the window!" Fresh scents and birds' songs poured through.

"Lie on your back and take deep breaths. That's what Dickon does when he's lying on the moor. He says he feels it in his veins, and he feels as if he could live forever."

Mary was describing the changes in the garden when the nurse came in. She was startled to see the window open. "Are you sure you're not chilly, Master Colin?" she enquired.

"No, I'm taking long breaths of fresh air. It makes you strong."

When the nurse returned with breakfast, Colin said in a Rajah-like manner, "A boy, and a fox, and a crow, and two squirrels and a newborn lamb, are coming to see me this morning. I want them brought upstairs," he said.

Within about ten minutes, Mary held up her hand. "Listen! He's coming!" Dickon's moorland boots made a clumping sound as he walked through the long corridors. He came in with a wide smile. The newborn lamb was in his arms and the little red fox trotted by his side. Nut sat on his left shoulder, Soot on his right, and Shell's head and paws peeped out of his coat pocket.

Colin sat up and stared with wonder and delight. Colin had never talked to a boy in his life and was so overwhelmed that he felt shy.

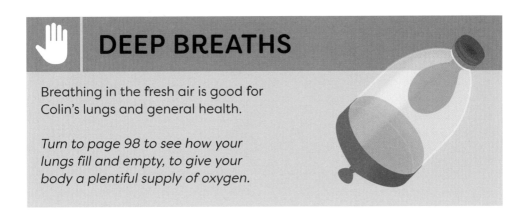

DEEP BREATHS

Breathing in the fresh air is good for Colin's lungs and general health.

Turn to page 98 to see how your lungs fill and empty, to give your body a plentiful supply of oxygen.

ACCENTS AND DIALECTS

An accent is the way someone pronounces words, while a dialect is the way someone uses vocabulary and grammar, as well as their pronunciation. Accents can vary according to how, when, and where you learned your language, as well as the people you regularly talk to.

When humans are in a group, they tend to dress, behave, and talk in a similar way. Everyone has an accent, even if they don't think they do! Sometimes, you can pick up an accent if you're surrounded by different people.

Yorkshire was once ruled by the Vikings. The Yorkshire accent Dickon and Martha speak has its origins in Old English and Old Norse. Some Yorkshire dialect includes "mardy" (moody), "nowt" (nothing), and "snicket" (alleyway).

Dickon walked over to Colin's chair and put the newborn lamb quietly on his lap, and immediately the little creature turned to the warm velvet dressing-gown and began to nuzzle.

"What's it doing?" cried Colin.

"It wants its mother," said Dickon, smiling. He took a feeding-bottle from his pocket. "Come on, little'un," he said. "This is what tha's after. There now," and he pushed the rubber tip of the bottle into the nuzzling mouth and the lamb began to suck it ravenously.

By the time the lamb fell asleep, Colin had so many questions. While they talked, Soot flew solemnly in and out of the window, while Nut and Shell scampered into the big trees outside. Captain curled up near Dickon, who sat on the hearthrug.

They looked at the pictures in the gardening books and Dickon knew all the flowers by name and knew which ones were already growing in the secret garden. "I'm going to see them!" Colin cried.

But they were forced to wait more than a week before they could visit the secret garden again, as the weather had turned and Colin was threatened with a cold. Mr. Roach, the head gardener, was startled one day when Master Colin summoned him.

It was a good thing Mrs. Medlock had warned Mr. Roach about the menagerie of animals. When he opened the bedroom door, a large crow seemed to announce his entrance. Colin was sitting in an armchair and a young lamb was standing by him, shaking its tail. A squirrel was perched on Dickon's bent back, and the little girl from India was sitting on a big footstool looking on.

"Oh, you're Roach, are you?" Colin said. "I have some very important orders. I'm going out in my chair this afternoon. If the fresh air agrees with me, I may go out every day. When I go, none of the gardeners are to be anywhere near the Long Walk by the garden walls. I shall go out about two o'clock and everyone must keep away until I send word that they may go back to their work."

"Very good, sir," replied Mr. Roach, with relief it wasn't a harder task.

Dickon went back to the garden with his creatures and Mary stayed with Colin. She didn't think he looked tired, but he was very quiet during lunch. "I can't help thinking about what the springtime will look like," he said. "I've never really seen it before."

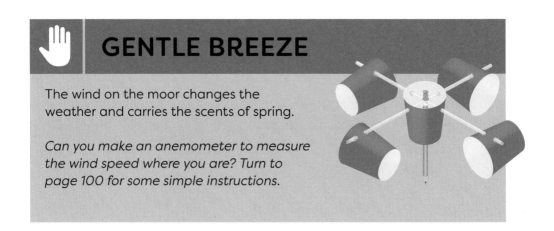

✋ GENTLE BREEZE

The wind on the moor changes the weather and carries the scents of spring.

Can you make an anemometer to measure the wind speed where you are? Turn to page 100 for some simple instructions.

"I never saw it in India because there wasn't any," said Mary. And they talked and talked about all the exciting things that lay ahead.

A little later, the nurse dressed Colin and the strongest footman carried him downstairs and put him in his wheeled chair while Dickon waited outside.

Dickon began to push the wheeled chair slowly and steadily. Mary walked beside it and Colin leaned back and lifted his face to the sky. The arch of it looked very high and the small snowy clouds seemed like white birds floating on outstretched wings. Colin kept lifting his thin chest to draw in the breeze.

"There are so many sounds of singing and humming and calling out," he said. "What is that scent the puffs of wind bring?"

"It's gorse on th' moor that's openin' out," answered Dickon. "Eh! Th' bees are at it wonderful today."

MAKE A LUNG IN A BOTTLE

When Colin takes deep breaths of fresh air into his lungs, he feels much better. Discover how your lungs fill and empty with this simple experiment.

1

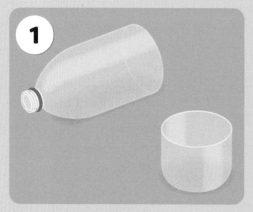

Ask an adult to help you cut off the end of the plastic bottle, as shown.

YOU WILL NEED:

- large plastic bottle
- 2 balloons (one red, one blue)
- scissors

2

Cut off the top of the blue balloon. Tie a knot at the bottom end.

3

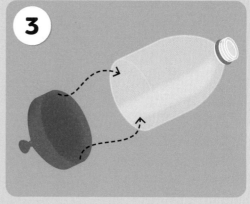

Gently pull the blue balloon over the large end of the bottle, as shown.

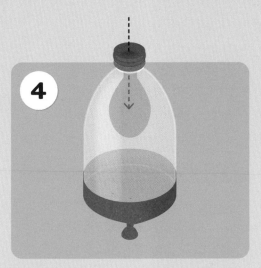

4 Take the red balloon and feed it into the bottle neck. Secure by folding the end of the balloon over the neck, as shown.

5 Gently pull down on the blue balloon. What do you notice about the red balloon?

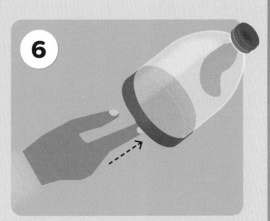

6 Now push the blue balloon back up. What do you notice this time?

WHY IT WORKS

The plastic bottle represents your chest, the red balloon represents one of your lungs, and the blue balloon represents your diaphragm. When you pull down on the blue balloon the "diaphragm" contracts, which increases the volume inside the bottle. This lowers the air pressure in the red balloon and causes more air to be drawn into the bottle/red balloon. When you push the blue balloon back up again, the "diaphragm" relaxes. This reduces the volume inside the bottle, forcing air out again.

MAKE AN ANEMOMETER

The wind on the moor can be a gentle breeze or a howling gale. Make an anemometer and watch how the wind strength changes its movement.

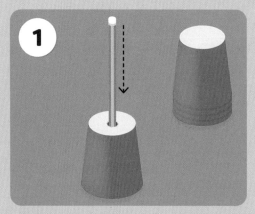

1

Ask an adult to help you pierce a hole in the bottom of one of the cups, using the pencil.

YOU WILL NEED:

- 5 paper cups
- hole punch
- 2 long straws
- pencil with eraser
- drawing pin

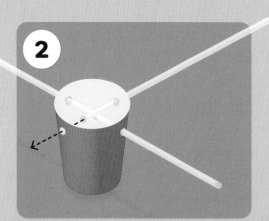

2

Punch four holes in the same cup, just below the rim as shown. Push the straws through these holes, overlapping in the middle.

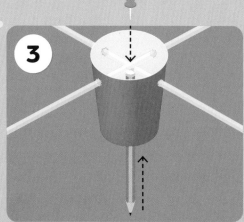

3

Push the pencil through the first hole (eraser side up) and fix loosely by pushing the drawing pin through the straws and into the eraser. Check your anemometer spins freely.

Punch two holes in each of the remaining cups, as shown.

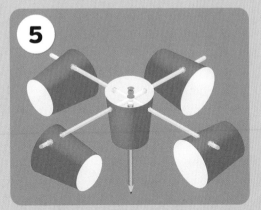

Thread the cups onto the straws through these two holes. The cups should all face the same way.

Hold your anemometer outside on a windy day (or use a fan inside). As the wind speed changes, watch the cups speed up and slow down.

WHY IT WORKS

Anemometers measure wind speed. The cups rotate as the wind blows and this turns the central rod. The anemometer spins more quickly in a strong wind, and the device counts and records the number of turns.

Chapter 8

Magic

When they reached the ivied walls, they began to speak in whispers.
"This is it," breathed Mary. "This is where the robin flew over the wall.
And that is where he showed me the key. This is the ivy the wind
blew back!" and she took hold of the hanging green curtain. "Here is
the handle, and here is the door. Dickon, push him in quickly!"

Colin covered his eyes with his hands until they were inside.
He found himself surrounded by splashes of color all around,
fluttering wings and humming and scents. Mary and Dickon stared
at Colin in wonder. A pink glow of color had crept over him.

"I shall get well!" he cried out. "And I shall live forever!"

Mary and Dickon worked a little here and there while Colin watched.
Then Dickon pushed the chair around the garden, stopping to show
Colin wonders springing out of the earth or trailing from the trees.
They drew the chair under the plum tree and Dickon had just drawn
out his pipe when Colin saw something he'd not noticed before.

"That's a very old tree, isn't it?" he said.

Dickon and Mary looked and there was a moment of stillness.
"Yes," answered Dickon, in a gentle voice.

"It's quite dead, isn't it?" Colin went on. "It looks as if a big branch has broken off. I wonder how it was done."

"It's been done many a year," answered Dickon. And with a sudden relieved start he laid his hand on Colin. "Look at that robin! There he is! He's been foragin' for his mate."

The robin darted through the greenness and out of sight. Colin leaned back on his cushion again, laughing a little.

"It was Magic that sent the robin," Mary said to Dickon secretly afterward. "I know it was Magic." For both she and Dickon had been afraid Colin would ask more about the tree.

Watching the robin carry food to his mate was making the children hungry. Colin suggested they ask for tea to be brought to the rhododendron walk. The hot tea and buttered toast and crumpets went down very well. "I don't want this afternoon to end," Colin said. "I've seen the spring now and I'm going to see the summer. I'm going to see everything grow here. I'm going to grow here myself."

✋ CHAIR WITH WHEELS

Mary and Dickon help Colin to explore the garden in his wheeled chair.

Can you make a wheelchair and take it for a spin? Turn to page 112 for some guidance.

"That tha' will," said Dickon. "Us'll have thee walkin' about here an' diggin' same as other folk afore long. When tha' stops bein' afraid tha'lt stand on thy legs."

Everything was still, so it was rather startling when Colin exclaimed in a loud whisper, "Who's that man? Look!"

Ben Weatherstaff's indignant face was glaring at them over the wall from the top of a ladder! He shook his fist at Mary.

"I never thowt much o' thee!" he shouted. "Allus askin' questions an' pokin' tha' nose where it wasna' wanted."

"Wheel me over there!" Colin said. "Stop right in front of him!"

"Do you know who I am?" Colin demanded.

"Aye, that I do—wi' tha' mother's eyes starin' at me out o' tha' face. But tha'rt th' poor cripple," replied Weatherstaff in disbelief.

Colin forgot that he ever had a weak back. His face flushed scarlet and he sat bolt upright.

THE SPEED OF SOUND

The children hear Ben Weatherstaff shouting over the garden wall. The sound of his voice is carried through the air.

We hear sounds when something makes a vibration and creates sound waves. Big vibrations make loud sounds and small vibrations make quiet sounds. Sound needs a material to travel through, such as a solid, liquid, or gas. That's why sound doesn't travel through the vacuum of space (where there is no air).

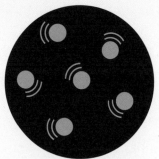

Molecules in gas

The speed of sound in air (a gas) is about 1,080 feet (330m) per second. Sounds travels about four times faster through water (a liquid), and even faster in solids. This is because molecules that are closer together pass on the vibrations more quickly. The speed of sound can also be affected by temperature. Molecules have more energy when they're at higher temperatures, which means they vibrate more quickly.

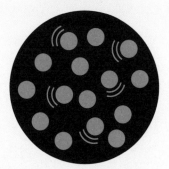

Molecules in liquid

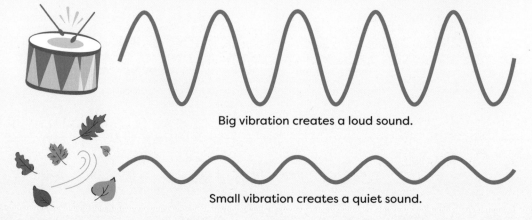

Big vibration creates a loud sound.

Small vibration creates a quiet sound.

"I'm not a cripple!" he cried furiously. Colin's anger and insulted pride filled him with an almost unnatural strength.

"Come here!" he shouted to Dickon, as he began to tear the coverings off his legs.

There was a brief scramble, the rugs were tossed to the ground, Dickon held Colin's arm and before long, he was standing upright, as straight as an arrow and looking strangely tall.

"Look at me!" he flung up at Ben Weatherstaff. "Just look at me!"

Ben Weatherstaff was choked with tears and he struck his hands together.

"Eh!" he burst forth, "tha'lt make a man yet. God bless thee!"

"When my father is away, I'm your master," Colin said, "and you're to obey me. Miss Mary will bring you here. We didn't want you, but now you'll have to be in on the secret. Be quick!"

"I can stand!" Colin said proudly to Dickon, as they waited.

"I told tha' could as soon as tha' stopped bein' afraid," answered Dickon. "An' tha's stopped."

"Are you making Magic?" Colin asked sharply.

Dickon grinned, "Tha's doin' Magic thysel'," he said. "It's same Magic as made these 'ere work out o' th' earth," and he gently touched a clump of crocuses with his thick boot.

"I'm going to stay standing when Weatherstaff comes. I can rest against the tree if I like."

When Ben Weatherstaff came through the door, he heard Mary muttering something under her breath. "What art sayin'?" he asked.

But she didn't tell him. She was saying to Colin, "You can do it! I told you, you could!" because she wanted to make Magic and keep him on his feet like that. And he did not give in.

"Look at me!" he commanded. "Am I a hunchback? Have I got crooked legs?"

"Nowt o' th' sort," Ben Weatherstaff said. "What did tha' shut thysel' up for?"

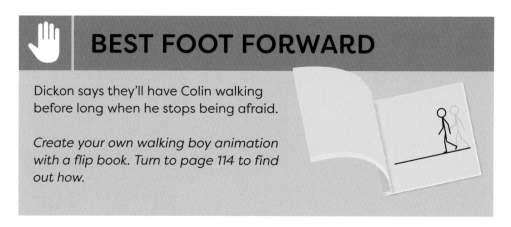

✋ BEST FOOT FORWARD

Dickon says they'll have Colin walking before long when he stops being afraid.

Create your own walking boy animation with a flip book. Turn to page 114 to find out how.

"Everyone thought I was going to die," Colin answered. "But I'm not! This is my garden now. I shall come every day. I may send for your help, but it must remain a secret."

"I've come here before when no one saw me," Ben said. "I came over th' wall. Th' rheumatics held me back th' last two year'."

"Tha' come an' did a bit o' prunin'!" cried Dickon.

"She says to me once, 'if ever I'm away you must take care of my roses.' When she did go away th' orders was no one was ever to come nigh. But I come an' did a bit o' work. She'd gave *her* order first."

When they returned to the house, Dr. Craven had been waiting some time. "You must not overexert yourself," he said.

"I'm not tired at all," said Colin. "It's made me well. Tomorrow, I'm going out in the morning as well as in the afternoon."

"I'm not sure I can allow it," answered Dr. Craven. "I'm afraid it wouldn't be wise."

"It wouldn't be wise to try to stop me," said Colin quite seriously.

After Dr. Craven had gone, Mary chastised Colin for being rude. "Nobody ever dared to do anything you didn't like—because they thought you were going to die. Always having your own way has made you so rude."

PRUNING PLANTS

Gardeners prune (cut back) the branches, leaves, and dead matter on plants. This is done for several reasons.

Pruning can make a plant look more attractive by helping to keep its size and shape. Removing dead or diseased wood helps to prevent disease from spreading and encourages strong new shoots to grow.

Pruning also helps flowers and fruit to grow. Pruning reduces the amount of stems or wood, which means the plant can put more energy into making flowers and fruit.

Pruning also increases the air flow around a plant and allows sunlight to reach the leaves and fruit. Pruning usually takes place once a plant has flowered.

"I don't want to be rude," said Colin. "I shall stop being rude if I go to the garden every day. There's Magic in there—good Magic."

The next morning in the garden, Colin sent for Ben Weatherstaff. "I want you and Dickon and Mary to stand in a row and listen to me because I'm going to tell you something very important. When I grow up, I'm going to make great scientific discoveries and I'm going to begin now with this experiment.

"Magic is a great thing and scarcely anyone knows about it. I believe Dickon knows some Magic—he charms animals and people. I'm sure there's Magic in everything, only we don't get hold of it and make it do things for us.

"Since I've been in the garden, I've had a strange feeling of being happy, as if something were pushing and drawing in my chest and making me breathe fast. The Magic has made me stand up and given me hope. I'm going to try to get some and make it push and draw me and make me stronger. Every day I'm going to say, 'Magic is in me! Magic is making me well!' And you must all do it, too. That's my experiment. Will you help?

"You learn things by repeating them over and over and thinking about them until they stay in your mind forever. If you keep calling Magic, it will get to be part of you and it will do things. We must only think of the Magic!"

MAKE A WHEELCHAIR

Colin explores the garden in his wheeled chair.
Make a wheelchair of your own and take it for a ride!

1

Cut a rectangular piece of cardboard the length of your doll from head to foot, and a little wider than your doll.

YOU WILL NEED:

- cardboard
- scissors
- small doll
- ruler
- 2 wooden skewers
- paper straws
- glue gun

2

Put your doll in a comfortable sitting position. Starting your "chair" at the doll's shoulder, bend the cardboard at the waist and knees. Bend at the foot as well to make a footrest.

3

Cut four circles of cardboard 3 inches (7cm) diameter. Ask an adult to help you pierce a small hole in the middle of the circles. Then glue pairs of circles together to make two strong wheels.

4

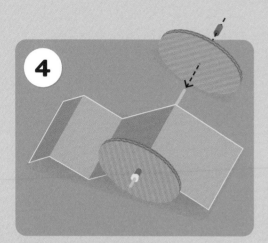

Glue a wooden skewer to the front of the seat, as shown. This is your axle. Add your wheels, cut the axle to size, and glue a small piece of straw to each end to secure.

5

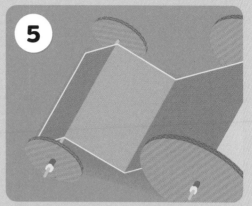

Repeat with a smaller set of wheels, about 1.5 inches (4cm) diameter. This time attach the axle to the front of the footrest, as shown.

6

Now you can push your wheelchair along wherever you choose!

WHY IT WORKS

Wheelchairs are designed with big wheels at the back and small wheels at the front. The big wheels often have a metal ring, to allow the user to turn (or stop) the wheel with their hands. Because the wheel is big, less force is needed to turn it. The small wheels at the front are "caster wheels" (like the wheels of a shopping trolley). They help the wheelchair to turn in different directions without much effort. They are small enough to turn, but large enough to cope with bumpy ground.

MAKE A FLIP BOOK

Mary and Dickon are determined to help Colin walk again. You can make Colin walk too with this simple animated flip book.

1

Hold the pack of sticky notes, with the sticky side on the left. Draw a pencil figure on the right-hand side of the last page, using this template as a guide.

YOU WILL NEED:
- pack of sticky notes
- pencil
- black pen

2

Once you are happy, draw over the image in black pen. Draw a line beneath the two feet. This will be your guide line.

3

Turn over a page, and trace your guide line. Now draw the next step of your boy walking, as shown here.

4 Draw over your outline in black pen as before.

5 Repeat for the last three steps, as shown here.

6 Flip through your sticky notes. You can repeat the steps if you want your boy to walk a little farther!

WHY IT WORKS

A flip book is a type of simple animation, also known as a kineograph or thumb book. The drawings in a flip book show the different stages of a particular movement, which change very gradually from one page to the next. When these pages are flipped quickly, they give the impression of movement. Movies use a similar format—a series of still images are played in quick succession to give the impression of movement.

Chapter 9

The Portrait

It all seemed most majestic and mysterious when they sat down in a circle. Dickon held his rabbit in his arms, and the crow, the fox, the squirrels, and the lamb slowly drew near. "The creatures have come," said Colin gravely. "They want to help us."

Colin really looked quite beautiful, Mary thought. He held his head high and his eyes had a wonderful look in them as the light shone through the tree canopy. "Now we'll begin," he said. "I will chant."

"The sun is shining—the sun is shining. That is the Magic. The flowers are growing—the roots are stirring. That is the Magic. Being alive is the Magic—being strong is the Magic. The Magic is in me. It's in every one of us. Magic! Come and help!" The humming of the bees mingled with the chanting voice, and he repeated it a great many times.

"Now I'm going to walk around the garden," he announced. They formed a procession, which moved slowly with dignity. Colin leaned on Dickon's arm, his head held high. "The Magic is in me!" he kept saying. "The Magic is making me strong!"

It seemed very certain that something was upholding and uplifting him. He sat down occasionally but would not give up until he'd walked around the whole garden. When he returned to the plum tree, his cheeks were flushed and he looked triumphant. "I did it. The Magic worked!" he cried. "That is my first scientific discovery."

"What will Dr. Craven say?" asked Mary.

"He won't say anything," Colin answered, "because no one will tell him. This is to be the biggest secret of all. No one is to know anything about it until I can walk and run like any other boy. I shall come here every day in my chair, and I shall be taken back in it. Then when my father returns to Misselthwaite, I'll just walk into his study and say 'Here I am; I'm like any other boy,' and I'll live to be a man."

"He'll think he's in a dream," cried Mary. "He won't believe his eyes!"

Before long, the children agreed that Dickon's mother could "come in on the secret." So one beautiful evening at home, Dickon told her the whole story.

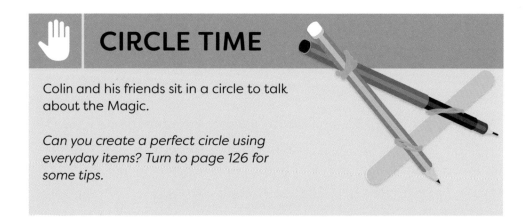

✋ CIRCLE TIME

Colin and his friends sit in a circle to talk about the Magic.

Can you create a perfect circle using everyday items? Turn to page 126 for some tips.

"My word!" she said. "Standin' on his feet! What do they make of it at th' Manor— him being so well an' cheerful an' never complainin'?" she asked.

"They don't know what to make of it," Dickon replied. "But he has to do his bit o' complainin' to keep them guessin'. The doctor tried to write to Mester Craven about th' improvement but Mester Colin said it would only disappoint him if he got worse again. Colin's savin' th' secret to tell himself.

"Although they don't know how to get enough to eat without makin' talk. If Mester Colin keeps sendin' for food they won't believe he's an invalid at all."

"I'll tell thee what, lad," Mrs. Sowerby said. "When tha' goes to 'em in th' mornin's tha' shall take a pail o' good new milk an' I'll bake 'em a crusty cottage loaf or some currant buns. Then they could take th' edge off o' their hunger while they were in the garden."

"Eh, mother!" said Dickon, "what a wonder tha' art! Tha' always sees a way out o' things!"

There was a riot of surprised joyfulness the morning Dickon went behind the big rose bush and brought forth two tin pails—one full of rich new milk with cream on top, and the other full of hot currant buns. What a kind, clever woman Mrs. Sowerby was!

YEAST

Yeast is a tiny microorganism that can be used to make bread rise. When you mix flour, water, and yeast together, the yeast reacts with the starch and sugar in flour to release carbon dioxide.

When you knead the dough, air bubbles become trapped in the mixture. Carbon dioxide from the yeast goes into these air bubbles, causing the dough to rise.

Yeast uses the energy it gets from sugars to reproduce, making the dough rise even further. Most bread recipes suggest you leave your dough to rise before you bake it.

When the bread is baked, it has a lighter texture. In contrast, unleavened bread is a type of flat bread made without the use of yeast.

Dough before rising

Dough after rising

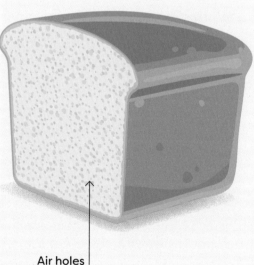

Air holes

"Magic is in her just like Dickon," said Colin. "It makes her think of ways to do such nice things. She is a Magic person. Tell her we are grateful, Dickon—extremely grateful."

This was the beginning of many agreeable incidents. They were aware Mrs. Sowerby already had fourteen people to feed, so they asked her to let them send some of their shillings to buy things. Dickon also found a hollow in the woods where you could build a stone oven and roast potatoes and eggs in it.

Every morning, the mystic circle met under the plum tree. After the ceremony, Colin always took his exercise and he grew stronger and could walk more steadily. His belief in the Magic grew stronger, too.

Dickon showed him some muscle exercises he'd learned from a man on the moor, and they soon became a part of the daily routine. Thankfully, the basket of provisions each day satisfied their growing appetites. But Dr. Craven and the nurse were mystified.

"They are eating next to nothing," the nurse said, "and yet, see how they look." Dr. Craven was puzzled. He looked at Colin long and carefully. "I'm sorry to hear you do not eat anything," he said. "That will not do. You will lose all you have gained."

It was all Mary could do to keep herself from laughing.

"Is there any way those children could be getting food secretly?" Dr. Craven inquired of Mrs. Medlock later.

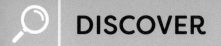

MUSCLES AT WORK

The skeletal muscles in your body help your body to move. You use them to bend and straighten your arms and legs, for example, and to bend your fingers to grip.

Skeletal muscles can only pull in one direction, so they come in pairs. A muscle contracts to move a bone but another muscle is needed to move it back again. When one muscle contracts, the other relaxes, and vice versa.

Skeletal muscles are called "voluntary" muscles because your brain can tell them when to move. Examples of muscle pairs include the biceps and triceps (in your arm) and the hamstrings and quadriceps (in your legs).

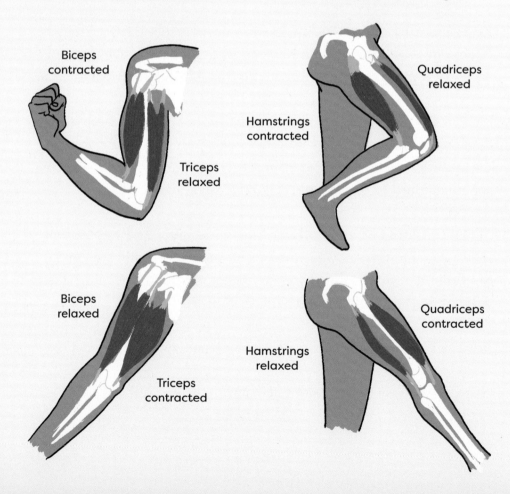

Biceps contracted

Triceps relaxed

Quadriceps relaxed

Hamstrings contracted

Biceps relaxed

Triceps contracted

Hamstrings relaxed

Quadriceps contracted

"Not unless they dig it out of the earth or pick it off trees," Mrs. Medlock replied. "They stay out in the grounds all day and see no one but each other."

"Well, so long as going without food agrees with them, we need not worry too much."

The secret garden bloomed and every morning revealed new miracles. The robin's mate was keeping her eggs warm in the nest. The robin had been watching the proceedings in the garden. He was wary at first of the new boy who came in a chair and who walked in a strange manner and needed to rest. Then the robin remembered when he learned to fly, he'd done the same sort of thing, taking short flights and then resting. Perhaps the boy was learning to fly—or rather to walk.

Even on wet days, Mary and Colin were never dull. One morning, when the rain streamed down incessantly, Mary had an idea. "Colin, do you know how many rooms there are in this house?"

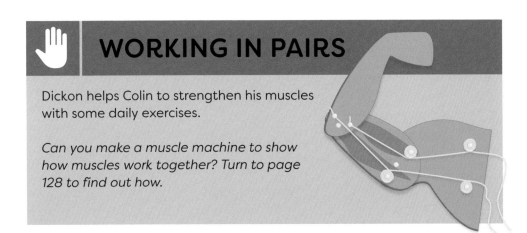

✋ WORKING IN PAIRS

Dickon helps Colin to strengthen his muscles with some daily exercises.

Can you make a muscle machine to show how muscles work together? Turn to page 128 to find out how.

"About a thousand, I suppose," he answered.

"There's about a hundred no one ever goes into. Suppose we go and look at them. I could wheel you in your chair and nobody would dare follow us. There are galleries where you could run. There are all sorts of rooms."

"Ring the bell," said Colin.

When the nurse came in, he said, "I want my chair. Miss Mary and I are going to look at the part of the house that is not used. John can push me as far as the picture-gallery because there are some stairs. Then he must go away and leave us alone until I send for him again."

Later, when they reached the picture-gallery, Colin and Mary looked at each other, delighted. "I'm going to run from one end of the gallery to the other," Colin said, "and then I'm going to jump and do my exercises."

They did all these things and more. They found endless portraits, including one of a plain little girl dressed in green brocade, holding a parrot on her finger.

"All these must be my relations," said Colin. "That parrot one, I believe, is one of my great, great, great, great aunts. She looks rather like you, Mary—when you first came. Now you're much prettier."

They found new corridors and corners and flights of steps. It was a curiously entertaining morning and the feeling of wandering about in the same house with other people but at the same time feeling as if one were miles away from them was a wonderful thing.

"I never knew I lived in such a big, old place. Let's ramble about every rainy day!"

That afternoon, Mary noticed that the curtain had been drawn back on the picture over the mantelpiece. "I know what you want me to tell you," Colin said. "I drew the curtain back because it doesn't make me angry any more to see her smiling. I want to see her smiling like that all the time now. I think she must have been a sort of Magic person perhaps."

"You are so like her now," said Mary, "that sometimes I think perhaps you're her ghost made into a boy."

"If I were her ghost, my father would be fond of me," he said. "If he grew fond of me, I think I should tell him about the Magic. It might make him more cheerful."

MAKE A DRAWING COMPASS

The children sit in a circle to help Colin with his experiment. Make your own "drawing compass" to create a perfect circle.

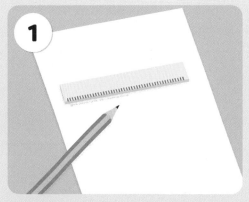

1

Decide how big you want your circle to be. Measure and draw the radius of your circle. This will be half the distance from one side of the circle to the other.

YOU WILL NEED:

- sheet of printer-size paper
- ruler
- sharp pencil
- pen
- thick elastic band
- 2 thin elastic bands
- wooden craft stick

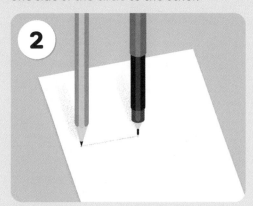

2

Hold your pencil tip at one end of the radius line and your pen tip at the other end of the radius line, as shown.

3

Keeping the pencil and pen tips in place, cross the pen and pencil over, as shown, and secure with the thick elastic band.

Place the wooden craft stick between the pencil and pen, as shown, and secure with the two thin elastic bands.

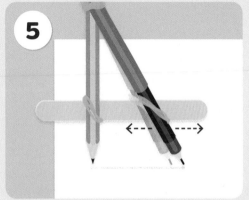

You can adjust the compass by sliding the elastic band along the craft stick. Use your original radius line as a guide.

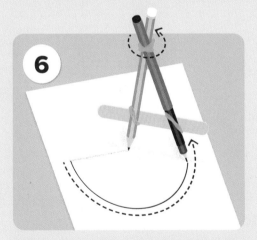

Now draw a perfect circle. Then change the radius to draw a bigger or smaller shape. You may find it easier to hold the compass in place and rotate the paper around it.

WHY IT WORKS

A compass can be used to draw circles or arcs (parts of circles). The sharp pencil helps to keep the compass in place. A circle is a series of points joined up, all the same distance from the center. These points form the perimeter (or circumference) of the circle. The distance from the center of the circle to the perimeter is called the radius. A line that passes through the center of the circle is called the diameter.

MAKE A MUSCLE MACHINE

Colin is strengthening his muscles with gentle exercises. Make this muscle machine to show the biceps and triceps muscles in action.

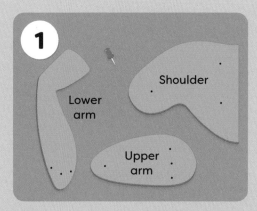

1

Shoulder

Lower arm

Upper arm

YOU WILL NEED:

- cardboard
- pencil
- scissors
- sheet of red paper
- glue
- drawing pin
- 8 butterfly clips
- 4 plastic bobbins
- string

Use these templates to draw and cut out the three different parts of the arm in cardboard. Use the drawing pin to mark the holes, as shown

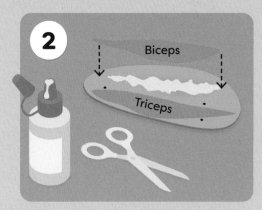

2

Biceps

Triceps

Now draw and cut out the two muscle shapes on red paper, as shown, and glue to the oval-shaped arm piece.

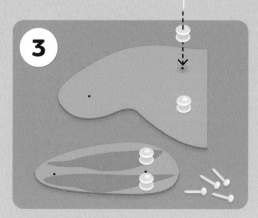

3

Use four butterfly clips to fasten the four plastic bobbins, as shown.

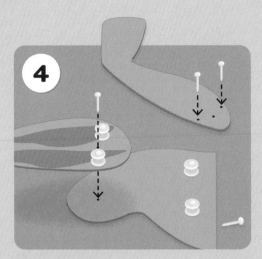

4

Now connect the "shoulder" to the "upper arm" with a butterfly clip and add two butterfly clips to the lower arm, as shown.

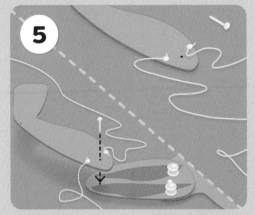

5

Cut two pieces of string about 18 inches (45cm) each. Tie a loop on each end and attach to the butterfly clips on the lower arm, as shown. Then secure the lower arm to the upper arm with the last butterfly clip.

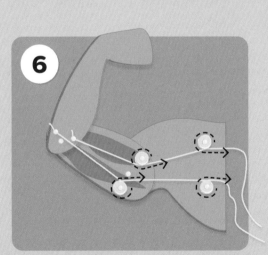

6

Thread the string through the bobbins, as shown, with the loops going in opposite directions. Hold the top of the shoulder and pull on the top string to move the arm up and pull on the bottom string to move the arm down.

WHY IT WORKS

The biceps and triceps muscles work together to help you bend your elbow. When you pull the top string to lift your arm, the biceps muscle contracts (shortens) and the triceps muscle relaxes and is pulled longer. When you pull the bottom string to lower your arm, the triceps muscle contracts and the biceps muscle relaxes and is pulled longer.

Chapter 10

Revealing the Secret

Their belief in the Magic was unwavering. During the magic circle each morning, Ben Weatherstaff noticed Colin's legs seemed straighter and stronger each day and his eyes had begun to hold a familiar light.

"The Magic works best when you work yourself," Colin said one morning. "You can feel it in your bones and muscles. I feel so well! And I shall never stop making Magic."

As they worked and laughed and talked together, Colin couldn't have been happier. Then something attracted his attention, and his expression became startled. "Who's coming in here?" he said quickly.

The door had been pushed gently open and a woman had entered. She had wonderful affectionate eyes that seemed to take everything in. No one felt she was an intruder at all.

"It's mother!" Dickon cried. He ran toward her and the others followed. "I knowed tha' wanted to see her an' I told her where th' door was hid."

"Even when I was ill, I wanted to see you," Colin said, "you and Dickon and the secret garden. I'd never wanted to see anyone or anything before."

Mrs. Sowerby flushed and a mist seemed to sweep over her eyes.

"Eh! Dear lad!" she said emotionally.

"Are you surprised because I'm so well?" he asked.

She put her hand on his shoulder. "Aye, that I am!" she said "but tha'rt so like thy mother tha' made my heart jump."

Then she put both hands on Mary's shoulders. "An' thee, too!" she said. "I'll warrant tha'rt like thy mother too. Mrs. Medlock heard she was a pretty woman. Tha'lt be like a blush rose when tha' grows up, my little lass, bless thee."

They took Mrs. Sowerby around the garden and showed her every bush and tree that had come alive. Colin walked on one side and Mary on the other.

"Do you believe in Magic?" Colin asked.

"That I do, lad," she answered.

"Suddenly I feel different—with my strong arms and legs and being able to dig and stand. I keep wanting to jump up and shout out," he said.

Dickon brought Mrs. Sowerby's basket from its hiding place and she watched them devour their food as they sat under the tree, laughing and joking. She was full of fun and made them laugh at all sorts of things. She told them stories in broad Yorkshire and taught them new words.

They also talked of visiting her cottage, where they would lunch outdoors and see all the children and wouldn't come back until they were tired.

Soon it was time for Colin to be wheeled back to the house. Before he got into his chair, he stood close to Mrs. Sowerby and caught hold of the fold of her apron. "You are just what I wanted," he said. "I wish you were my mother—as well as Dickon's!"

Mrs. Sowerby bent down and drew him to her with her warm arms, as if he'd been Dickon's brother. The quick mist swept over her eyes.

"Eh! Dear lad!" she said. "Thy own mother's in this 'ere very garden, I believe. She couldna' keep out of it. Thy father mun come back to thee—he mun!"

POSITIVE THINKING

Colin's mindset has changed since he visited the garden. He feels more confident in the things he can do and happier about his future. Positive thinking has helped to change his emotions.

Can you create a paper rose full of positive and inspiring thoughts? Turn to page 140 for some simple instructions.

It's true that thoughts can be as good for one as sunlight or as bad for one as poison. If you let a sad thought stay in your mind, it's like letting a germ get into your body. Mary used to be a sickly child. But when her mind filled itself with robins and springtime, there was no room left for the disagreeable thoughts that made her sour and tired.

So long as Colin thought only of his fears and weakness, he let himself be an invalid. When new beautiful thoughts crowded out the bad ones, life began to come back to him. His blood ran healthily and strength poured into him like a flood. It is said: "Where you tend a rose, my lad, a thistle cannot grow."

While the secret garden was coming alive, Mr. Craven was wandering in the mountains and valleys of Europe. For ten years, he'd kept his mind filled with dark thoughts and he'd forgotten and deserted his home and his duties. Until one day, a strange thing happened.

He was walking in an Austrian valley and stopped to rest by a beautiful stream. As he sat gazing into the clear water, Mr. Craven gradually felt his mind grow quiet. He began to notice the stunning surroundings that filled his mind with beauty. He did not know how long he sat there, but at last got up and drew a long, deep breath. Something seemed to have been released in him.

He remembered this strange moment many months afterward when he found out quite by chance that on this very day, Colin had cried out as he went into the secret garden, "I shall live forever!"

PARTS OF THE BRAIN

Your brain controls the way your body moves and how you think, feel, and remember.

The brain has three main parts. The largest part, the cerebrum, controls movement and is used for memory, thinking, and feeling.

The cerebellum controls balance and coordination. Lastly, the brain stem connects the brain to the spinal cord and controls bodily functions such as breathing, heart rate, and digestion.

The limbic system is found within the cerebrum. It controls our behavior and our emotional responses.

Studies have shown that negative thinking can affect the brain's ability to reason and think rationally, while positive thinking can free up the brain to work at its full potential.

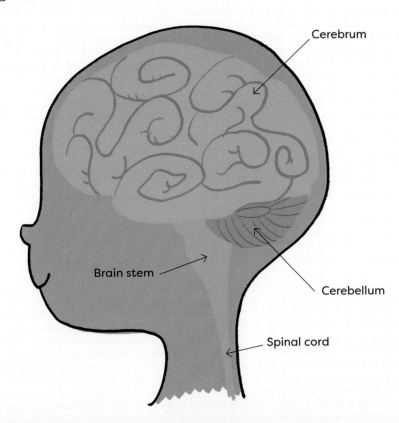

Cerebrum

Brain stem

Cerebellum

Spinal cord

Although Mr. Craven's dark thoughts returned from time to time, the blackness seemed to lift again. One night, he dreamed he heard a voice calling. "Archie! Archie!" it said.

"Lilias! Where are you?"

"In the garden!" it came back like a sound from a golden flute.

And then the dream ended, but he did not wake. He slept soundly all night until a servant woke him with his post. There was a letter from Yorkshire which simply said... ----

In a few days, Mr. Craven was in Yorkshire again and he felt a curious sense of homecoming crossing the moor. "In the garden!" he thought. "I must find the key."

"Please, sir, I would come home if I was you. I think you would be glad to come and—if you will excuse me, sir—I think your lady would ask you to come if she was here. Your obedient servant, Susan Sowerby."

"How is Master Colin?" he asked Mrs. Medlock when he arrived.

"Well, sir," she answered. "He's different. He likes to spend time outdoors, and he laughs a lot these days. He's in the garden, sir."

"In the garden," he repeated, almost as if he was in a trance. He felt like he was being drawn back to the garden and he didn't know why.

When he reached the ivied wall, he heard sounds of scuffling feet and suppressed voices coming from inside the garden. Was he going mad?

MOMENTUM

When Colin flies through the door of the secret garden, it's difficult for him to stop! He tries to slow down but momentum carries him forward.

Momentum describes "mass in motion." The amount of momentum something has depends on how much is moving (its mass) and the speed at which it is moving (its velocity).

We write this as:
Momentum = Mass x Velocity

An object with momentum can be slowed down or stopped if a force is applied against it.

Brakes can slow down the speed of a moving vehicle. The faster the vehicle is traveling, the greater the braking force needed to slow it down. Colin is trying to win a race, so he's moving as fast as he can. When he comes through the door, his momentum is only slowed down by his father's arms.

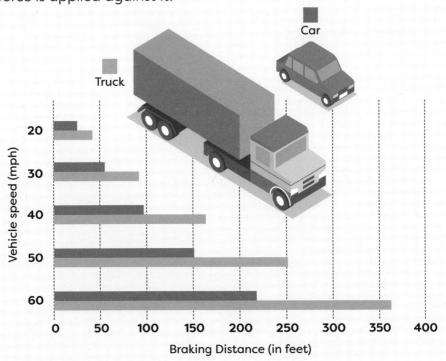

Truck

Car

Vehicle speed (mph)

20
30
40
50
60

0   50   100   150   200   250   300   350   400

Braking Distance (in feet)

And then the moment came. The feet ran faster, the door was flung wide open, and a boy burst through at full speed and almost dashed into his arms. Mr. Craven just saved him from falling, and when he looked in amazement, he truly gasped for breath.

He was a tall, handsome boy, glowing with life and his eyes were full of boyish laughter. It was the eyes which made Mr. Craven gasp.

This was not what Colin had planned. And yet to come dashing out after winning a race—perhaps it was even better. "Father," he said. "I'm Colin! You can't believe it. I scarcely can myself. I'm Colin."

"In the garden! In the garden!" Mr. Craven said hurriedly.

"Yes," continued Colin. "It was the garden that did it—and Mary and Dickon—and the Magic. We kept it from you so we could tell you when you came. I'm well and I'm going to live forever and ever!"

Mr. Craven's soul shook with unbelieving joy as he put his hands on the boy's shoulders and held him still. He knew he dared not even try to speak for a moment.

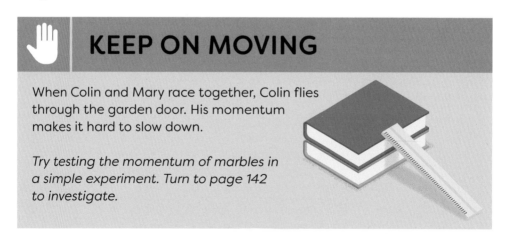

✋ KEEP ON MOVING

When Colin and Mary race together, Colin flies through the garden door. His momentum makes it hard to slow down.

Try testing the momentum of marbles in a simple experiment. Turn to page 142 to investigate.

"Take me into the garden, my boy," he said at last. "And tell me all about it."

As he looked around at all the autumn gold, purple, and violet blue, and flaming scarlet and climbing roses, he could hardly believe it. "I thought it would be dead," he said.

"Mary thought so at first," Colin said, "but it came alive." And he told his father the whole story. "Now, it need not be a secret anymore. I shall walk back with you, Father—to the house."

When Mrs. Medlock caught sight of the lawn, she threw up her hands and gave a little shriek and every man and woman servant within earshot bolted across the servants' hall and stood looking through the window with their eyes wide.

Across the lawn came the Master of Misselthwaite and he looked a new man. And by his side was a boy with eyes full of laughter, who walked as strongly and steadily as any boy—Master Colin!

THE END

MAKE A PAPER ROSE

Colin is feeling more positive since he visited the secret garden. Create a paper rose full of positive thoughts to brighten up your day.

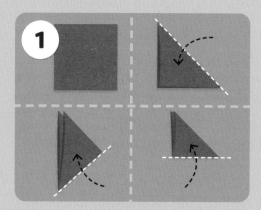

Fold one piece of red paper in half diagonally, and fold two more times to make a small triangle. Repeat with the three other pieces of paper.

YOU WILL NEED:

- 4 sheets of red paper (4x4 inches or 10x10cm)
- pencil
- scissors
- small coin about 1 inch (25mm) across
- glue
- green pipe cleaner

Draw around the coin on the triangle, as shown, and cut out. Snip the very end from the triangle. Repeat with the three other triangles of paper.

Open out your "petals." On the first, cut out one segment. On the second, cut out two segments, and so forth.

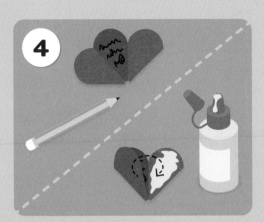

Take the 3-segment petal. Write a positive thought on the middle segment and glue the outside segments together. Press out into a cone shape. Repeat with each larger petal, writing positive thoughts on the middle segments and gluing the outside segments together.

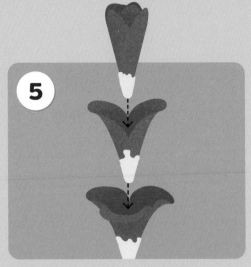

Use your pencil to gently roll out the top of each petal, as shown. Roll the single segment petal up tightly, glue and roll this within the 2-segment petal. Now glue each petal into a bigger cone, as shown, until you have your finished flower.

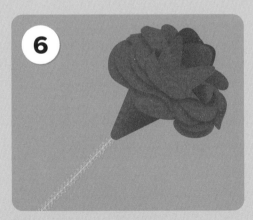

Ask an adult to help you push the green pipe cleaner through the bottom of your rose, and secure in place.

WHY IT WORKS

Wild roses have just five petals but cultivated roses can have up to 40! Rose petals are sometimes used to make perfume and also for medicinal purposes. Positive thoughts are good for your mental health, too. If you see the positive in things, you'll feel better about life and more able to deal with any worries. You'll also find that positive thinking attracts positive people, bringing happiness and friendships to your days.

EFFECTS OF MOMENTUM

Colin finds it hard to slow down because the running race has increased his momentum. Try this experiment to investigate how mass and speed affect the momentum of marbles.

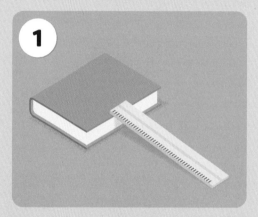

1

Take one hardback book and rest the ruler on the top, as shown.

YOU WILL NEED:

- 2 hardcover books
- ruler with a groove in the middle
- second ruler
- masking tape
- piece of cardstock 4 inches long
- 2 marbles (one small, one large)
- paper and pencil

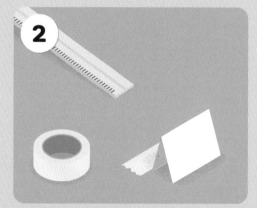

2

Fold the cardstock in half and stand it up a little way in front of the ruler, as shown. Mark this place on your table with some masking tape.

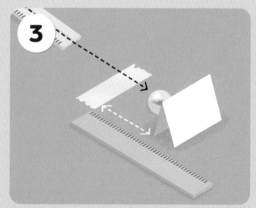

3

Hold the small marble at the top of the ruler and let it roll down. It should push the cardstock as it falls. Mark the position of the cardstock with masking tape and use your second ruler to measure the distance it's traveled.

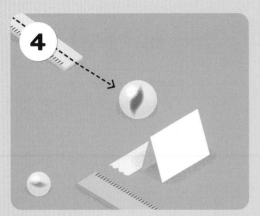

Reposition your cardstock to its original position and try the experiment again using the large marble. How far does the cardstock travel this time?

Now repeat the experiment using two hardcover books on top of each other—with the small marble and then the large marble. What happens each time?

Repeat each experiment a few times and make a table of your findings. Calculate the average distance each marble travels. How does the momentum differ?

WHY IT WORKS

You should find that when the marbles travel from the height of one book, they have less momentum. When the marbles travel from the height of two books, the force of gravity makes them travel faster and they push the cardstock farther away. The large marble also has more momentum because it is heavier.